James Payn

The Kenton Cook-Book

James Payn

The Kenton Cook-Book

ISBN/EAN: 9783744781282

Printed in Europe, USA, Canada, Australia, Japan

Cover: Foto ©Andreas Hilbeck / pixelio.de

More available books at **www.hansebooks.com**

—THE—

KENTON COOK-BOOK

PUBLISHED BY THE

KENTON COOK-BOOK CO.

> Their various cares in one great point combine,
> The business of their lives—that is, to dine.
> —*Love of Fame.*

> The turnpike road to people's hearts, I find,
> Lies thro' their mouths, or I mistake mankind.
> —*Peter Pindar.*

W. M. BECKMAN,
KENTON, OHIO.

Entered according to Act of Congress, in the year 1888, by
THE KENTON COOK-BOOK CO.,
In the Office of the Librarian of Congress, at Washington.

The Publisher's Compliments to the Reader.

DEAR MADAM:

The ladies of St. Paul Episcopal church who publish this book, for the purpose of raising enough money for furnishing their new church, have spent much time in preparing the following recipes for substantial and dainty dishes. All have been thoroughly tested by the ladies whose names are attached. They hope that as a result of their use, you will recommend its purchase to your friends.

CONTENTS.

Soups.
Fish
Oysters
Meats
Meat and Fish Sauces
Poultry and Game
Entrees
Eggs
Salads
Sandwiches
Vegetables
Breads
Pies and Puddings
Sauces for Puddings
Desserts
Cakes
Beverages
Preserving
Pickles and Catsup
Candies
Miscellaneous
Things Worth Knowing
Dinner Giving
Menus

PREFACE.

I have been requested by some fair women of Kenton to contribute a preface to a cook-book that is to aid in its sale the building of an Episcopal Church. I could as well be asked to put up a prayer, or preach a sermon, in the church after it is dedicated. Nevertheless I comply.

It has been tersely said by a French scientist that man is to be distinguished from other animals by the fact that he cooks. I cannot say that this is correct, for cooking does not come, like Dogberry's reading and writing, by nature; and so far as our instinctive nature goes we share it with the buzzard. This scavenger leaves the sun to do its cooking, and we let decay go far enough to make meat tender, before we add the artificial process of cooking to complete the work. That definition of man—that he is a laughing animal—is better, for we share that with the dog. The dog is nobler than the buzzard; in many respects it is nobler than man. True, the dog laughs with his tail, and man with his mouth. But all extremes meet, and from the mouths of some men to the tails of all dogs is no great distance. However, whether we are cooking animals or not, cooking has come in the evolution of humanity to be a necessity. We can not feed upon the raw material, although the latest reach of science in that direction is to fetch us very close to uncooked nature. The doctors prescribe raw steaks for invalids, while the canvass-back ducks are merely dressed and carried through the kitchen to the table, when perfectly prepared for the culinated taste of epicures.

This does not apply to ducks generally. I remember once, on a hunting expedition, we, the hunters, attempted to roast a duck. We followed the instruction of the cook book, and our duck was as tough as the conscience of a County Commissioner. A cynical old scoundrel, who had been looking on, said, "Boys, you don't know duck, and your cook book isn't worth a North Pacific toad." This was when those famous Cookes, of the North Pacific R-N- mess, failed. "Let me show you—nail your duck by the tail to your tent pole and let it hang there till it drops, then roast and eat." The gamey flavor of wood-cock and snipe comes from the same process. Frogs' legs are stringy if put on the griddle, or in the pan, kicking. They must first be subjected to what Byron sings of, as "decay's effacing fingers."

This is not the case, however, with terrapin, according to my genial old friend, the Hon. Beverly Tucker. That is not the Tucker referred to in the negro melody, who was too late for supper—it must have been in a chilly condition of atmosphere when dear old Bev. was left in that way. Bev. says the way to stew terrapin is to put the insects alive in cold water, place them over a slow fire, and stew for an hour. This is good for epicures, but bad for terrapin. One can imagine the surprise of the living delicacies to find the water warming, and how they disported themselves in the genial liquid, then, as it grew rather too warm, their disgust at the Signal Office that had not foretold the warm wave, and their wonder as to when it would moderate, and so on until the extreme heat ended in wrathful indignation and death.

Putting aside these philosophical speculations, and coming down to practical facts, the dear, sweet girls of Kenton ask me for a preface to their cook book, that like Liberty—not West Liberty, but New York Liberty—is not only to enlighten the world, but aid in building an Episcopal Church at their town. I am the last man in the world to ask for such a work. Some years since, my liver awakened me to the fact that I have a stomach, and when that happens to any one it is a farewell, a long farewell, to faring well in that direction. Ah me! Our life begins with a deadly attack on that part of our body where we live. The poor infant is lifted into that infernal invention, called a high chair, and permitted to swallow all the indigestion of the table that would kill alligators. The tender little stomach is poisoned. Small wonder that over half of the human family die in childhood, and only the tougher and coarser live on to afflict each other with dyspepsia, the seeds of which are planted in the high chair.

A woman is taught everything on earth but the proper care of children. This is considered indelicate, and so it is omitted from homes and boarding schools. How to catch a husband, through finished extremities, is the aim of all training and instruction of girls.

However this valuable and practiced work is not food for babies, but strong meat for men. As such it must be prized and practiced upon in order that we may learn the truth of the maxim of Chas. Granmiller, "the stomach is the source of enjoyment of life;" and avoid the blessing indulged in by Charles Lamb, who was wont to ask when requested to solicit one, "Is the cock about? No; then let us be thankful."

MAC O-CHEE.   DONN PIATT

ERRATA.

Page 17   In Broiled Oysters,—*thin* slices instead of *three* slices.
Page 20   In Oyster Pie.—*stirring* instead of *thinning*.
Page 27   Broiled Pork *Chops* instead of Broiled Pork *Roasted*.
Page 27   In White Sauce,—*stir* instead of *steam*.
Page 30   Chicken *Sauté* instead of Chicken *Sauce*.
Page 33.   In Sweet-breads –*parboil thirty minutes* after draining off water.
Page 34   In Broiled Sweet-Breads.—A *pair* instead of a *pan*.
Page 35   In Larded Sweet-breads—*one teacupful* bread crumbs.
Page 35   In Larded Sweet-Breads,—A *pair* instead of a *pan*.
Page 73   In Mince Meat,—Boiled *cider* instead of *vinegar*.
Page 76   In Raisin Pudding—*two cupfuls* of raisins.
Page 94   In Caramel Ice Cream—*one quart* of boiling cream
Page 102   In Vanity Cake—*whites four eggs*.
Page 103   In Ginger Drop Cake—*two eggs*.
Page 104   In Cream for Layer Cake—one *pint* of milk.
Page 108   In French Cake—*three eggs*.
Page 111   In Washington Cake—one cupful of *butter*, not *water*.
Page 112   *Custard* not *Mustard* Cream Cake.
Page 115—In Columbia Cake—*four eggs*.
Page 123—In Canned Peaches—add more *sugar* instead of *eggs*.
Page 124   In Ax Jar Pickles—mix turmeric with cold *vinegar*.
Page 127   Chocolate Creams,—*cake* instead of *sack*.
Page 127   In Chocolate Creams—*one cupful* of water.

SOUP.

HOW TO MAKE SOUP.

Buy a good sized Soup-Bone, about equal amount of bone and meat, have the bone well broken at the meat market and all fat removed. Put into a kettle of cold water, a quart of water to a pound of soup-bone; let it simmer gently for half an hour, then boil slowly for five or six hours. An hour before taking from the fire, put in a good sized potato, a carrot and an onion. When done strain through the colander and set away in a cool place. The next day skim off all the fat, the stock should then be the consistency of jelly. It is now ready for use. In the winter it will keep for a week; in warm weather, three days if kept in a cool place. Every range should have a soup-pot, into which can be thrown trimmings of fresh meat, bones and pieces of meat left from roast and broils (when not the least scorched); the stock will not be so clear as one can obtain from a soup-bone, but is as rich in flavor. Never throw away the smallest bone, save for the soup-pot. Stock is also valuable for sauce, gravies and stews. Each day before dinner it is only necessary to cut off some of the stock and heat it. Always adding aside from the thickening, salt, celery salt, a little catsup or Worcestershire sauce.

Have hot water in soup tureen. Never remove soup from the range unless at a boiling point. As nothing is more unpalatable than half warmed soup. Serve each guest one ladle full of soup.

Mrs. Innes.

THICKENINGS FOR SOUP.

To thicken with flour—Put a small piece of butter in a cup and when boiling add sifted flour, boil well together, then add to the soup.

To thicken with tapioca—Soak tapioca two or more hours in cold water, then boil until like jelly, add to the soup.

Vermicelli is to be added a few minutes before removing the soup from the fire.

Macaroni should be boiled tender before adding to soup

If you wish to flavor with tomato, add before using thickening.

Rice and barley should be boiled tender before adding to soup. as it is only necessary to cook soup-stock a few minutes before serving.

BOUILLON.

Heat clear soup-stock, add pepper, salt, celery salt, cloves, a little catsup or Worcestershire sauce, port or sherry to suit the taste. Serve in cups for breakfast and luncheon. When used for dinner call Consomme, and serve in soup-plates.

Egg-Dice, Bread-Dice, and Force-meat balls are put in the tureen, and the hot soup is poured over them. Of course only one kind is used at a time.

EGG DICE.

Two eggs, two tablespoonfuls of milk, one-fourth teaspoonful of salt. Beat eggs with a spoon, add milk and salt. Turn into a buttered cup and place in a pan of warm water. Cook in a slow oven until firm in the center. Set away to cool. Cut into dice.

Mrs. Montgomery.

FORCE-MEAT BALLS.

Chop some veal, one-fourth as much butter as veal, season with salt, pepper, a few drops of lemon juice. Bind with a raw egg, some crackers or bread crumbs. Roll into small balls and fry brown in boiling lard.

Miss Hoge.

BREAD DICE.

Take stale bread and cut in dice, fry brown in hot butter; allow to cool before dropping into the soup tureen.

Mrs. Innes.

NOODLES.

To three eggs well beaten, add two tablespoonfuls of water and a little salt; enough flour to make stiff dough. Work well for fifteen minutes, adding flour when necessary. When pliable cut off a portion at a time, roll very thin, sprinkle over flour, and beginning at one side, roll into rather a tight roll. With a sharp knife cut it from the end into very thin slices. Let them dry an hour or two. Cook in the soup about ten minutes.

Miss Hoge.

MOCK BISQUE SOUP.

A quart can of tomatoes, three pints of milk, a large tablespoonful of flour, butter the size of an egg pepper and salt to taste, a scant teaspoonful of soda, a pinch of cayenne. Put the tomato on to stew and the milk in a double boiler to boil, reserving half a cupful to mix with flour. Mix the flour smoothly with this cold milk, stir into the boiling milk and cook ten minutes. To the tomato add the soda; stir well, and rub through a strainer that is fine enough to keep back the seed. Add butter, pepper, salt to the milk and then the tomato. Serve immediately.

POTATO SOUP.

A quart of milk, six large potatoes, one stalk of celery, an onion and two small tablespoonfuls of butter. Put milk to boil with onion and celery. Pare potatoes and boil thirty minutes, turn off the water, mash fine and light. Add boiling milk and butter, pepper and salt to taste. Rub through a strainer, and serve immediately. A cupful of whipped cream should be added when in tureen.

CREAM OF CELERY SOUP.

A pint of milk, a tablespoonful of flour, one of butter, a head of celery, a large slice of onion and small piece of mace. Boil celery in a pint of water from thirty to forty-five minutes, boil mace, onion and milk together. Mix flour with two tablespoonfuls of cold milk, and add to boiling milk. Mash celery in the water in which it has been cooked and stir into boiling milk, add one pint chicken or veal stock, butter, pepper and salt to taste.

MISS HOGE.

BLACK BEAN SOUP.

A pint of black beans, soaked over night in three quarts of water. In the morning pour off this water, and add three quarts of fresh. Boil gently six hours. When done there should be one quart. Add a quart of stock, six whole allspice, a small piece of mace, a small piece of cinnamon, a stock of celery, a boquet of sweet herbs, also two small onions and one small slice each of turnip and carrot, all cut fine and fried in three tablespoonfuls of butter. Into the butter remaining in the pan put a spoonful of flour and cook until brown. Add to soup and simmer all together one hour. Season with salt and rub through a fine sieve. Serve with slices of lemon and egg balls, the lemon to be put in the tureen with the soup.

TOMATO SOUP.

One quart can of tomatoes, one pint of water, and a slice of an onion, let simmer thirty minutes. Mix one tablespoonful of flour and one of butter with a tablespoonful of the tomato; stir into the boiling mixture, add one-half teaspoonful of salt and a pinch of cayenne. Let all boil for fifteen minutes, strain through a sieve, and serve immediately.

MRS. W. S. ROBINSON.

OYSTER SOUP WITH MILK.

Boil one quart of rich milk, season with pepper, salt and a large tablespoonful of butter, then add one quart of oysters and just let it come to the boiling point, and serve.

Miss Hoge.

OYSTER SOUP WITH WATER.

One pint of oysters and one quart of boiling water, let boil five minutes, then skim out the oysters. Add a pint of fresh oysters, pepper, salt to taste, two tablespoonfuls of butter and one of rolled cracker. Bring to the boiling point and serve.

Miss Robinson.

WHITE BEAN SOUP.

Soak a quart of navy beans over night. Then put on the fire with three quarts of water, three onions fried or *sauted* in a little butter, one small carrot, two potatoes partly boiled in other water, a small piece of pork, a little red pepper and salt. Let it all boil slowly for five or six hours, then add one quart of stock. Strain through a colander. Return the pulp to the fire, season with salt and pepper. Put bread-dice in the tureen and pour over the soup.

Mrs. Robinson.

CHICKEN SOUP.

One chicken for a gallon of water. Cut up chicken and place in cold water then let it boil for five or six hours. Strain through a colander and set aside until the next day, when the fat will be ready to skim off and the stock like jelly. Fifteen minutes before dinner put the jelly on the fire; when it comes to a boil add a pint of cream or milk. Thicken with a little flour which has been stirred smooth with a tablespoonful of cold milk, season with salt and pepper. Just before taking up the soup pour in a cupful of thoroughly cooked rice. Some like a few drops of onion juice.

Mrs. Innes.

This soup must be taken off the fire at a boiling point.

The bones and meat left from a roast chicken make nice chicken stock for this same soup.
Mrs. Innes.

THE JOHN CARLIN SOUP.

Three pints of stock, one pint of tapioca after it is cooked to a jelly consistency. (Soak tapioca over night.) Season with salt, pepper and celery salt, Worcestershire sauce and tomato catsup. When the soup is in the tureen, drop in slices of lemon, one for each plate. Take the soup from the fire at a boiling point.
Mrs. Innes.

OXTAIL SOUP.

Take two oxtails, an onion, two carrots, two stalks of celery, a little parsley and a small cut of pork. Cut the oxtails at the joints, slice the vegetables and mince the pork. Put the pork, onion and oxtails into a stewpan and fry them a short time. Now put the oxtails and fried onions into soup kettle, with four quarts of cold water. Let simmer for about four hours; then add the other vegetables, with four cloves, pepper and salt. As soon as the vegetables are well cooked, the soup is done. Strain it.
Miss A. Powell.

FISH.

BROILED FISH

Any small fish, and the steaks of very large fish are nice broiled. Dry the fish with a coarse cloth, rub the bars of the gridiron with lard to prevent the fish from sticking. Put the fish in broiler and turn often. A fish weighing three pounds will broil in ten minutes. Season with pepper, salt and melted butter. Garnish with lemon and parsley. A double broiler is better. Be careful that the fish does not scorch.
Miss Robinson.

BAKED HALIBUT.

Take a piece of halibut weighing five or six pounds, and lay in salt and water for two hours. Wipe dry and score the outer skin. Set in the baking pan in a tolerably hot oven, and bake an hour, basting often with butter and water heated together in a tincup or sauce pan. When a fork will penetrate it easily it is done. It should be a fine brown. Take the gravy in the dripping pan, add a little boiling water. Should there not be enough, stir a tablespoonful of catsup, the juice of a lemon and thicken with browned flour, previously wet with cold water. Boil up once and put into sauce boat.

Mrs. W. S. Robinson.

BAKED FISH.

Clean, wash and wipe the fish, which should be a large one. Make a stuffing of grated bread-crumbs, butter, salt, pepper and sweet herbs. Stuff the fish and sew it up. Lay in the baking pan, with a cupful of water to keep it from burning, and bake an hour, basting with butter and water until it is tender throughout and well browned. Take it up, put in a hot dish and cover tightly, while you boil up the gravy with a great spoonful of catsup, a tablespoonful of browned flour which has been wet with cold water, the juice of a lemon, and if you want to have it very fine a glass of sherry. Of course you take out the thread with which it has been sewed up before serving the fish.

Mrs. W. S. Robinson.

STEAMED FISH.

A five pound fish should be steamed one hour or longer until thoroughly done, as there is nothing more unwholesome than under-done fish. Wash it in cold water, then wrap in a cloth and put into the steamer. It will not break the fish to curl it up when when putting into the steamer. Serve with caper sauce. If the fish is to be served whole do not cut off the head and tail.

Mrs. Innes.

BROILED MACKEREL.

Soak over night in lukewarm water, change in the morning for very cold, let the fish lie in this until time to cook. Broil over a clear fire. Pour over melted butter, sprinkle with pepper, and serve with sliced lemon.

Miss Hoge.

SPICED MACKEREL.

Soak half a dozen mackerel over night, boil until tender, remove bones and lay in a stone jar. Boil one quart of vinegar with one grated nutmeg, three blades of mace and three cloves; pour over the fish. Will be ready for use in about two days.

Mrs. A. Letson.

TURBOT.

Two pounds of white fish. Steamed until done, remove bones while hot. Set away to cool. One and one-half pints of milk, four tablespoonfuls of butter, pepper and salt; boil and add chopped parsley. Set away to cool. Butter turbot dishes, fill with layers of fish and dressing, sprinkle top with bread or cracker-crumbs, little butter, pepper and salt.

Mrs. Innes.

CODFISH BALLS.

Seven ordinary sized potatoes and the same amount of fish picked up very fine. Boil potatoes, and a little while before draining put in the fish. Let all come to a boil, drain and mash together, add one egg and a small piece of butter. Let cool and then make into finger rolls and drop into boiling lard. They must brown quickly so as not to soak up the lard. Let the codfish soak over night in cold water.

Mrs. Childs.

STEWED CODFISH.

Pick the codfish very fine, soaking in cold water over night, in the morning drain off water and simmer gently ten minutes, pour off water, and dress with milk, or cream if you have it, butter, a sprinkling of flour, pepper and salt. Pour into center of a good sized meat plate garnished with mashed potatoes.

Mrs. Innes.

OYSTERS.

OYSTER SAUTÉ.

Drain one quart of oysters on a coarse cloth; season with salt and pepper. Put slices of bacon to cover the bottom of a hot skillet, and let it fry until brown. Put oysters in same pan and cook, turning each oyster. Serve on squares of buttered toast. Garnish with slices of bacon and parsley.

Mrs. Carlin.

BROILED OYSTERS.

Lay large oysters on a close gridiron. Cook on one side, then on the other. Season with pepper, salt and melted butter. Serve on squares of toast, and garnish with three slices of lemon.

Miss Robinson.

STEAMED OYSTERS.

Lay some oysters, in the shell, on a steamer. Set over a pot of boiling water until the shells open. Serve at once with salt, pepper and butter. Lemon can also be used.

OYSTERS IN THE SHELL.

Open the shell, melt some butter, with pepper and salt, roll the oysters in it and lay back in the shells, putting more than one oyster in each shell if you wish, cover with bread crumbs and small pieces of butter. Place in pan and set in oven. Serve in the hot shells with lemon.

Mrs. Robinson.

OYSTER CHARTREUSE.

One quart of oysters, one pint of cream, one small slice of onion, half a cupful of milk, whites of four eggs, two tablespoonfuls of butter, salt, pepper, two tablespoonfuls of flour, one cupful of fine, dry bread crumbs, six potatoes, one tablespoonful of minced parsley. Pare and boil potatoes, mash fine and light, add the milk, salt, pepper, one tablespoonful of butter and then the whites of the egg beaten to a stiff froth, and the parsley Have a two quart Charlotte Russe mould well buttered and sprinkle the bottom and sides with bread crumbs, (there must be butter enough to hold the crumbs). Line the mould with the potato and let stand a few minutes. Put the cream and onion on to boil, mix the flour with a little cold cream or milk,—about one-fourth of a cupful—and stir into the boiling cream. Season well with salt and pepper and cook eight minutes. Let the oysters come to a boil in their own liquor, skim them and drain off all the juice. Take the onion from the sauce and add the oysters. Taste to see if seasoned enough, and turn into the mould very gently, cover with the remainder of the potato, being careful not to put on too much at once. When covered bake half an hour in a hot oven. Take from the oven ten minutes before dishing time, and let it stand on the table. It should be baked half an hour. Place a large platter over the mould and turn both dish and mould at the same time. Remove the mould very gently. Garnish the dish with parsley and serve. A word of caution. Every part of the mould must have a thick coating of mashed potato and when the covering of potato is put on no opening must be left for sauce to escape.

OYSTER FRITTERS.

Drain the liquor from the oysters, and to a cupful of this add one half a cupful of milk, three eggs, pinch of salt, and flour to make a thin batter. Have in a frying pan some butter smoking hot, drop in the batter by the spoonful. Fry brown and serve *very* hot.

FRIED OYSTERS.

Drain and wipe oysters dry. Beat an egg with a little milk, pepper and salt, dip oysters into the egg, then into rolled cracker or bread crumbs. Fry in a kettle of hot lard or put butter in skillet and let get hot, then fry oysters a delicate brown.

LITTLE PIGS IN BLANKETS.

Season large oysters with pepper and salt. Cut fat English bacon in very thin slices. Wrap an oyster in each slice and fasten with a little wooden skewer (toothpicks are best). Heat a frying pan and put in the little pigs. Cook just long enough to crisp the bacon—about two minutes. Place on slices of toast cut into small pieces and serve immediately. Garnish with parsley.

ROAST OYSTERS.

Eighteen large oysters or thirty small ones, one teaspoonful of flour, one tablespoonful of butter, salt, pepper and three slices of toast. Have the toast buttered and on a hot dish. Put the butter in a small saucepan, and when hot add the dry flour. Stir until smooth, but not brown, then add one and a half cups of cream and let it boil up once. Put the oysters (in their own liquor) into the hot oven for three minutes, then add them to the hot cream, season and pour over the toast. Garnish the dish with thin slices of lemon. Serve hot. A nice dish for lunch or tea.

Mrs. W. S. Robinson.

PANNED OYSTERS.

Drain the oysters in a colander. Have a fryingpan very hot, pour in the oysters, a lump of butter size of an egg (for a pint of oysters), one tablespoonful of cracker crumbs, teaspoonful of lemon juice, salt and cayenne pepper. Let all cook together for a minute or so, just until the oysters commence to curl.

Mrs. Innes.

OYSTER PIE.

One quart of oysters, one pint of milk, one half pint of water, one half cupful of butter. Put milk, water and butter on stove and let get scalding hot, add one heaping tablespoonful of flour rubbed smooth in a little milk, and cook until it thickens. Add three eggs well beaten, then two tablespoonfuls of rolled cracker and the oysters and let scald, thinning all the time. Season with pepper and salt

Turn this into baked crust. For crust, make after rule for puff paste, line the baking dish and bake. Cut the upper crust to fit dish and bake on heavy paper if you haven't pan the right size. Prick the bottom crust with a fork to prevent it blistering.

MRS. GAGE.

SCALLOPED OYSTERS.

Drain the oysters. Put a thin layer of cracker crumbs in the bottom of a buttered pudding-dish, cover with a deep layer of oysters, season well with pepper, salt, and sprinkle with bits of butter. Add another layer of cracker crumbs, then oysters, pepper, salt and butter, and so on until the dish is full. Let the top layer be of crumbs, stick pieces of butter thickly over it, cover the dish, set in the oven, bake half an hour, remove cover, pour over half a cup of hot cream and set on the grate to brown. Use at least three-fourths oyster to one-fourth cracker. A little mace or nutmeg can be used in seasoning.

MISS HOGE.

MEATS.

HOW TO SELECT MEAT.

Good BEEF should be of a bright red color, the fat yellowish and firm. When the lean is streaked with the fat it indicates gradual fattening and is sure to be good. The fat should be a clear light yellow, a dull appearance shows a poor quality of beef.

Beef should be hung some time before using.

VEAL should have white fat and the lean be of a pinkish hue. White meat shows poor blood; and when too young, the lean is of a bluish color. Veal is not nutritious and is indigestible, but nothing can take its place for entrees and soups.

MUTTON should be a rather bright red, not too dark, and with plenty of hard white fat. It grows more tender by hanging.

LAMB will not keep as long as mutton; the bone should be rather red and the fat a clear white, the lean a light red almost pink.

CHICKEN. The light meat of chicken should be white, and the fat a light yellow. Young chicken have not much fat, and are best for broiling or smothering. When bending back the wing, of the skin cracks, the chicken is a young one. Chickens should be thoroughly chilled after killing, or they will be stringy.

MRS. W. S. ROBINSON.

ROAST BEEF.

See that the meat is of good color with plenty of fat. *Never* wash a roast of beef. Put the pan in which the roast is to be baked, on top of stove, and let get smoking hot. Take roast and sear on three sides in the hot pan. Season well with pepper and salt and put in a hot oven. Cook an eight pound roast from one and a half to one and three-fourth hours. The hour and a half will leave the center of the roast quite rare, but not raw. Baste often. Never put water in the pan while cooking. If the roast is not fat enough add some beef drippings or butter to baste with.

MRS. ROBINSON.

ROAST BEEF WITH YORKSHIRE PUDDING.

A rib or surloin roast should be prepared as directed for roasting. When within three-quarters of an hour of being done, have the pudding made. Butter a pan like that in which the meat is cooking and pour in the batter. Place in oven and baste occasionally with beef drippings. Cut in squares and garnish the beef with these. For Yorkshire pudding, one pint of milk, two-thirds of a cupful of flour, three eggs and one scant teaspoonful of salt will be needed, one teaspoonful of Royal Baking Powder. Beat the eggs very light, add salt and milk and then pour about half a cupful of the mixture on the flour and baking powder, and when perfectly smooth add the remainder. This makes a small pudding, enough for six persons. Serve hot.

Mrs. Innes.

BROILED BEEF STEAK.

Have the steak cut from three-quarters to an inch thick. Broil over a clear fire and turn constantly to keep from burning. When cooked season with pepper and salt. Many like melted butter poured over meat and pressed in. *Never* pound steak, as much of the juice is lost in that way. Is nice served with mushroom sauce or tomato sauce.

BEEF A-LA-MODE.

Take a round of beef, remove the bone from the middle, trim away the tough bits about the edges and the gristle. Bind the beef into a symmetrical shape by passing a strip of stout muslin around it. Have ready at least a pound of salt fat pork, cut into strips as thick as your middle finger and long enough to reach from top to bottom of the trussed round. Put a half pint of vinegar over the fire in porcelain sauce pan; season with two onions, two teaspoonfuls of made mustard, one teaspoonful grated nutmeg, one of cloves, half as much allspice, half teaspoonful of black pepper, with a bunch of sweet herbs minced fine, and a tablespoonful of brown sugar.

Let all simmer for five minutes, then boil up at once, and pour, while scalding hot, upon the strips of pork, which should be laid in a deep dish. Let all stand together until cold. Remove the pork to a plate, and mix with the liquor left in the dish enough breadcrumbs to make a tolerably stiff forcemeat. If the vinegar is very strong dilute with a little water before moistening the crumbs.

With a long-bladed knife or larding needle, make perpendicular incisions in the beef, not more than half an inch apart; thrust into these the strips of fat pork, so far down that the upper ends are just level with the surface, and work into the cavities with them a litle of the forcemeat. Fill the hole from which the bone was taken with the dressing and bits of pork. Put into a porcelain kettle with about half a pint of boiling water, cover the top of the meat with slices of carrot and turnip; cover the kettle tight and steam for four hours. Remove from the kettle and put in a baking-pan, roast for half an hour. Remove the muslin, and serve either hot or cold. Carve horizontally into very thin slices.

This seems like a good deal of trouble, but will find yourselves well repaid. MRS. S. L. HOGE.

ROAST VEAL.

Score the top of the roast and lay thin pieces of pickled pork where it has been scored. Season well with pepper and salt and put small pieces of butter over top and dredge with flour. Let cook until a little brown on top, add a half pint of boiling water and baste often. Cook a six pound roast from one and three-fourths to two hours. You may have to add a little boiling water again. If you care for gravy, make when the roast has been taken up. Put one-half pint of boiling water and one-half pint of cream in pan. Stir smooth two tablespoonfuls of flour in a little milk, add to water and cream while cooking, season with pepper and salt and cook *thoroughly*. MRS. ROBINSON.

ROAST PIG.

Prepare a dressing as for turkey, of fine bread-crumbs (about two quarts), a tablespoonful of salt, half a cup of butter, half a tablespoonful of pepper, one tablespoonful each of chopped parsley, thyme, and sage. Moisten with the yolks of two eggs, half a wine-glassful of sherry wine, the juice of half a lemon. This quantity will be sufficient for a six weeks' old pig. Salt and pepper the inside of the pig, fill with the dressing and having bent the legs under so that he will kneel, place in the pan with a well greased paper under. Rub the whole surface once with melted butter and dredge with flour (this keeps the skin from cracking). Put a half cup of hot water with some butter in the pan and set in a moderate oven. Have a pan of hot water and butter on the stove; baste the pig with this every ten minutes until the skin becomes quite brown, then stop basting but rub over the surface with a cloth dipped in melted butter. Do this *very* often, it will make the skin crisp and keep it from cracking. For an older pig double the quantity of dressing will be needed. Be sure your pig is *thoroughly* cooked. From three to four hours is not too much for a month old pig; six to eight hours for one three months old.

Mrs W. S. Robinson.

BROILED VEAL CHOPS.

Veal chops broiled are very nice. Have a steady heat and cook longer than beef or mutton. Season with pepper, salt and melted butter. Lemon juice is an addition. Garnish with parsley.

Miss Robinson.

VEAL CUTLETS, BREADED,

Dip the cutlets in beaten egg, with a little milk, pepper and salt added, then roll in cracker crumbs and fry in hot butter. Can be served with tomato sauce.

Mrs. Robinson.

BRISKET OF VEAL.

Get a loin roast of veal, make a dressing of bread crumbs, butter, salt, pepper and thyme or sage, and a little chopped pickled pork. Put this dressing on the under part of the veal, and roll, bind with a strip of muslin. Put into a pan with a little hot water, and bake, basting often. Cook a six pound roast from one and three-fourths to two hours. Make gravy as for roast veal.

Miss Hoge.

ROAST VEAL WITH RICE AND ONION.

Prepare veal the same as in above receipt, when about half done pour over the top rice and onion. Boil the rice until tender, five minutes before draining; put in two onions chopped fine, boil together for the five minutes, drain, stir well together, paste on top of veal, bake until veal is done.

Mrs. Damon.

VEAL SCALLOP.

Chop some cold roast or stewed veal very fine, put a layer in the bottom of a buttered pudding-dish, and season with pepper and salt. Have next a layer of cracker crumbs, sprinkle with bits of butter and moisten with a little milk, then more seasoned veal and another layer of cracker crumbs. When the dish is full wet with gravy or broth. Have a layer of crackers on top wet with milk and two beaten eggs. Bake from half to three-quarters of an hour. Do not get it too dry.

Miss Hoge.

ROAST SPRING LAMB.

Season the quarter of lamb with pepper, salt and spread thickly with butter, dredge with flour. If the meat is not fat lay thin pieces of pickled pork over it. After the meat has cooked thirty minutes add one-half cupful of water and baste often. Cook an eight pound roast two hours in a brisk oven to have well done. Serve with mint sauce.

Mrs. Childs.

BOILED FRESH TONGUE.

Wash well and put into boiling water to cover, with three tablespoonfuls of salt and one tablespoonful of pepper. Cook six hours or until very tender. Cook down in kettle, being careful that it does not burn. Peel off the skin while hot.

SMOKED TONGUE.

Soak over night and cook from five to six hours. Peel off skin while hot.

BROILED LAMB CHOPS.

Lamb chops are broiled as steak is broiled and served with salt pepper and melted butter. They are nice served with green peas.

BROILED MUTTON CHOPS.

Broiled as lamb chops are broiled. Many like them breaded and cooked like veal cutlets, and served with tomato sauce.

BOILED MUTTON.

Season the leg of mutton with pepper and salt and put in a kettle with just enough water to keep from burning, add a little water from time to time as needed. The rule is to boil a quarter of an hour for each pound of meat. Caper sauce should be served with this meat.

BOILED HAM.

Soak the ham over night in cold water. In the morning wash and scrape clean. Put into a kettle and cover with cold water and boil slowly. Allow fifteen minutes to each pound of meat in cooking. Put a few whole cloves and allspice into the water. When done remove from the kettle, and take off the skin. Cover the top of the ham with brown sugar, stick in a few cloves and set in the oven to brown. Do not cut until *cold* then slice very thin. Garnish the plate with parsley.

Mrs Hoge.

BROILED HAM.

Cut in slices; if salty, pour boiling water over the meat and let it stand five or ten minutes. Wipe dry and boil over a clear fire. Pepper before serving. If the ham looks dry, pour a little melted butter on it.

PORK ROASTED.

Season with pepper, salt, and sage. Add one-half cup of boiling water, baste often and allow twenty-five minutes to the pound for roasting. Have a moderate oven. Serve with apple-sauce. Many prefer a well seasoned bread crumb dressing.

BROILED PORK ROASTED.

Broil over a hot fire. Season with pepper and salt. Be sure to cook them enough.

MEAT AND FISH SAUCES.

WHITE SAUCE.

One quart of milk, four tablespoonfuls of butter, four of flour, a small slice of onion, two sprigs of parsley, salt and pepper to taste. Put the milk, onion, and parsley on the double boiler. Mix the butter and flour together until smooth and light. When the milk boils, stir four tablespoonfuls of it into the butter and flour, and when it is well mixed, stir it into the boiling milk, cook eight minutes. Steam and serve.

CREAM SAUCE.

One pint of cream, one tablespoonful of flour, salt and pepper to taste. Let the cream come to a boil, add the flour mixed smooth with a little cold cream; boil three minutes.

TOMATO SAUCE.

One quart of canned tomatoes, two and a half tablespoonfuls of butter, two of flour, ten cloves, and a slice of onion grated. Cook tomatoes, cloves, onion, ten minutes. Heat the butter in a pan and add the flour, stir over the fire until smooth and brown, then stir into the tomatoes. Cook two minutes, rub through a sieve, season with pepper and salt.

Miss Hoge.

MINT SAUCE.

Pour the grease off the drippings of roast lamb, add a tablespoonful of tomato catsup and some green mint chopped fine.

Miss Hoge.

MINT SAUCE.

Two tablespoonfuls of chopped green mint, one of powdered sugar, and half a teacupful of cider vinegar, stir all together and serve with roast lamb.

Miss A. Powell.

BUTTER SAUCE.

Two tablespoonfuls of flour, half a cupful of butter and one pint of boiling water. Work the flour and butter together until light and creamy, and gradually add the boiling water. Stir constantly until it comes to a boil, but do not let it boil. A tablespoonful of lemon juice and a speck of cayenne may be added if desired.

Mrs W. S. Robinson.

EGG SAUCE.

Six hard boiled eggs, chopped fine with a silver knife or spoon, half a cupful of boiling cream or milk and the butter sauce. Make the sauce, add the boiling milk and then the eggs. Stir well and serve. The juice of half a lemon makes this a sharp sauce. May add one tablespoonful of parsley.

ANCHOVY SAUCE.

Make the butter sauce and stir into it four tablespoonfuls of essence of anchovy, and one of lemon juice. Best for fish.

Mrs. W. S. Robinson.

CAPER SAUCE.

Make a butter sauce, and stir into it one tablespoonful of lemon juice, two of capers, and a speck of cayenne. This sauce is for stewed or boiled fish or mutton.

Mrs. W. S. Robinson.

BREAD SAUCE FOR GAME.

Two cups of milk, one-third cupful of fine dry bread crumbs, a slice of onion, one tablespoonful of butter, salt and pepper. Put the milk, bread crumbs and onion on to boil together. Boil fifteen minutes; add the butter and seasoning. Skim out the onion and pour around the birds or in a gravy boat.

Mrs. W. S. Robinson.

OYSTER SAUCE.

Make the cream sauce, and when boiling add one pint of oysters. Let them boil only just long enough to swell.

Mrs. W. S. Robinson.

MUSHROOM SAUCE.

Make the cream sauce, and when boiling add one pint of mushrooms cut into pieces. Let boil a few minutes.

POULTRY AND GAME.

CHICKENS BROILED IN A HOT OVEN.

Take spring chicken, have split open on back. Wipe perfectly dry. Put in baking pan and broil in very hot oven twenty five minutes. Season after removing from the fire with pepper, salt and melted butter. Garnish with thin slices of lemon and parsley.

Mrs Spelman.

SMOTHERED CHICKENS.

Flour, pepper and salt thoroughly spring chickens. Put a good sized lump of butter in the pan, and let it get hot on top of the stove. Put in the chickens breast downwards and brown, then put in the oven for about thirty minutes. Add then half a pint of water, cover with a pan, cook another thirty minutes, basting occasionally. Let them cook with breasts down until the water is added.

Mrs. Robinson.

CHICKEN SAUCE.

Cut up one uncooked chicken. Have ready a hot frying pan with a tablespoonful of butter in it. Place the chicken in the pan and brown, first on one side, then on the other. Season, cover tightly, set on the back of the stove, and cook slowly forty-five minutes.

Mrs Henry Powell.

ROAST CHICKENS.

Having picked and drawn them, wash in two or three waters, adding a little soda to the last. Prepare a stuffing of bread crumbs, butter, pepper, salt and a little onion. Fill the chickens, which should be young and tender, sew them up and roast an hour or more, according to their size. Baste often with butter and water, afterwards with their own gravy.

Miss Hoge.

STEWED CHICKEN.

Cover chicken with cold water, and when it boils skim well, then add pepper, salt and if chicken is not fat, add one-half cup of butter; let boil until tender. Stir until smooth two tablespoonfuls of flour with a little cold milk. Add a pint of cream, then the flour; let cook ten minutes and pour over buttered toast, baking powder, biscuit, or dumplings.

CURRIED CHICKEN WITH RICE.

Stew chicken as in above receipt. Place chicken on platter, garnish with rice. Stir curry powder to taste in gravy and pour over all.

ROAST TURKEY.

Proceed the same with turkey as with chicken, allowing fifteen minutes to a pound. Roast slowly and baste often. It is well to cover the breast with a well greased paper. Stuff the turkey with a dressing made of bread-crumbs, seasoned with pepper, salt, butter, onion, thyme or sage. Or mix oysters with the bread crumbs, or use oysters only. Another way, add raisins and sage to the bread-crumbs, and omit onion.

Miss Hoge.

BROILED SPRING CHICKEN.

Broil with the breast down about twenty minutes, baste with melted butter. Turn to keep from scorching.

Miss Hoge.

CHICKEN PIE.

Stew the chicken until tender, remove chicken, and add to the gravy pepper, salt, cream and flour, let it come to a boil. Place in your baking-dish first the back of the chicken, then the wings and any other pieces of chicken, and some small pieces of potato, then pour on some of the gravy. Have ready a rich baking-powder biscuit dough, roll out half an inch thick and put over the chicken, add the rest of the chicken, and cover again with the dough, cut a slit in the middle of the dough, pour the rest of the gravy through the slit. Place on the top of stove, cover lightly, and boil ten minutes; remove the cover and bake in the oven half an hour.

WILD DUCKS.

Clean the ducks and stuff the body with a dressing of bread crumbs seasoned with pepper, salt, melted butter, sage and onions, or a stuffing of onions alone. Fry the onions brown and season with pepper and salt. Place the ducks in a pan and pour about a half-pint of boiling water in the pan and baste often. Keep covered. If the ducks are young three-fourths of an hour or one hour will cook them long enough. When the ducks are old, they should be steamed an hour and then roasted thirty minutes. If the ducks are not fat, lay thin slices of bacon over breast.

Mrs. Robinson.

BROILED QUAIL.

Split them at the back. Broil, basting them often with butter, over a hot fire. As soon as the birds are done add a little more butter, pepper and salt. Can be served on buttered toast.

Mrs. Innes.

SMOTHERED QUAIL.

Smother quails after the receipt for chicken. Be careful to put the breast down in the hot butter and baste often; add more boiling water if necessary, as they must be kept moist.

Miss Robinson.

ROASTED SNIPE AND WOODCOCK.

The following is the epicure's manner of cooking them: Carefully pluck them, and take skin off the head and neck. Truss them with the head under wing. Twist the legs at the first joint pressing the feet against the thigh. Do not draw them, but tie a thin slice of bacon around each; run a small iron skewer through the birds, and tie it to a spit at both ends. Roast them at a good fire, placing a dripping pan with buttered slices of toast under them to catch the trail as it falls. Baste the snipe often with a paste-brush dipped in melted butter. Let them roast twenty minutes, then salt the birds and serve them immediately on toast.

The majority prefer snipe drawn and broiled, and served on toast.

PHEASANTS

Are cooked as quail, either broiled or smothered.

ENTRÉES.

TO FRY CROQUETTES.

Have a deep skillet or frying-pan for frying croquettes, and use plenty of pure, sweet lard, three-quarters to one pound is not too much. Have it boiling hot before dropping in the croquettes. When it smokes in the center it is just right.

SWEET-BREADS.

To clean sweet-breads, place them in cold water immediately on their arrival from market. In an hour drain off water, no matter what the mode of cooking is to be. After they are cold, pull off all the tough and fibrous skin.

MRS. INNES.

FRIED SWEET-BREADS.

Cut the sweet-breads into small pieces, after they are boiled and cold. Put a tablespoonful of butter into a frying-pan; when hot add sweet-breads, pepper and salt. The sweet-breads can be rolled in egg and cracker-crumbs before frying, if one wishes it.

MRS. INNES.

BROILED SWEET-BREADS WITH ORANGES.

Choose a pan of the largest sweet-breads; parboil; when cold, gash them in two or three places, then squeeze an orange carefully over them, so that the juice will run into the gashes; sprinkle with pepper and salt. Broil over the hot coals, basting frequently with melted butter. Squeeze the juice of another orange over them as they go to the table. Garnish with rounds of oranges. Lemons can be used in the same way.

Miss Hoge.

STEWED SWEET-BREADS.

After they are parboiled and cold, cut them up into fine pieces. Make a dressing of cream, thickened with flour; season with butter, pepper and salt; boil slowly for ten minutes, then add sweet-breads; cook five minutes longer, they are then ready to serve.

Mrs. Innes.

SWEET-BREAD CROQUETTES.

After they are well boiled, and cold, chop into very fine pieces, season with salt, cayenne pepper and celery salt; add sufficient cream to make *very* moist, roll in egg and cracker crumbs well sifted, and fry in hot lard to a light brown. They may be served alone or with pease or tomato sauce.

Mrs. Innes.

ROASTED SWEET-BREADS.

Parboil, then throw into cold water to harden. Wipe perfectly dry. Lay in a dripping-pan and roast, basting with butter and hot water (mixed), until they begin to brown. Then withdraw from the oven an instant, roll in beaten egg, then in cracker-crumbs; return to the oven for ten minutes longer, basting meanwhile with butter. Lay in a chafing dish while you add to the drippings half a cupful of hot water, some chopped parsley, a teaspoonful of browned flour, and the juice of half a lemon. Pour over the sweet-breads before sending to the table.

Miss Hoge.

CHICKEN CROQUETTES.

Boil one chicken until tender, and when cooked have about one cupful of broth When the chicken is cold divest it of all skin, fat and gristle, and chop as fine as possible. Put half a cupful of butter with two heaping tablespoonfuls of flour, rubbed smooth, into a saucepan and cook together, stirring constantly until as thick as cream; add the broth, after removing the fat, and a cupful of cream, boil five minutes. Take from the stove and add chicken, a little minced parsley, the juice of one lemon, salt, pepper, a very little cayenne, one half onion grated, one-fourth of a nutmeg, and set away to cool. When cold make into pear-shaped cones or little rolls, put into beaten egg, then the rolled cracker, and let stand about two hours before frying in hot lard. Veal, tenderloin of pork, and cold turkey can be used in place of chicken, and are very nice.

Mrs. Robinson.

BREADED CHEESE, For Tea or Luncheon.

One cup of coarse bread-crumbs, three cups of milk, one cup of grated cheese. Put into a pudding-dish with crumbs and butter on top. Bake thirty minutes.

Mrs. Innes.

LARDED SWEET BREADS.

Take a pan of sweet breads, soak one and a half hours in cold water; plunge in boiling water and cook five minutes. When cold and carefully skinned, make incisions through them one inch apart, into which insert tiny strips of salt pork and a little forcemeat made thus,—one teaspoonful of dry and finely rolled bread crumbs, one ounce of butter, the grated rind and juice of one lemon, one teaspoonful of finely chopped parsley; salt and pepper to taste. Put about a teaspoonful of this mixture in each incision; put bits of butter over the sweet-breads and bake to a pretty brown. Ten to fifteen minutes should cook them.

Miss M. W. Cumming.

POTATO CROQUETTES.

Season cold mashed potatoes with pepper, salt, nutmeg, and a little grated onion. Beat to a cream, with a tablespoonful of butter to every cupful of potato, add some minced parsley, and bind with two or three eggs. Roll into oval balls, dip into beaten egg, and then into cracker crumbs, rolled very fine, and fry in boiling lard.

Miss Hoge.

CHICKEN CROQUETTES.

For one dozen, use three-fourths of a pound of chicken cut fine, but not hashed, one-half a can of mushrooms also cut fine, one teaspoonful of grated onion, one tablespoonful of butter and one of flour, yolks of two raw eggs and a glassful of sherry. Put onion and butter in a sauce pan over the fire, and fry until the onion begins to color; then stir in the flour, the liquor from the can of mushrooms, and a scant cut of chicken broth, the chopped chicken, mushrooms, and a seasoning of salt, pepper, and a little grated nutmeg, and the sherry. Stir the mixture over the fire until it begins to boil, remove from the fire and stir in the eggs without beating them. Pour out the mixture on a dish, add a few drops of salad oil to keep from hardening while it cools. Form into finger-rolls, dip in egg and cracker crumbs, and fry in boiling lard.

Mrs. S. L. Hoge.

FRIED MUSHROOMS.

After removing stem and skin, wash them in two waters and throw into salted water and let stand one hour. Put butter in frying-pan and let get hot. Drain mushrooms from salt water throw into hot butter and let cook fifteen minutes, season with pepper. Pour on buttered toast. Always use silver spoon and if it turns black throw the mushrooms away.

OYSTER PATES.

Make a rich puff paste, roll very thin and line your small tins, prick your dough with a fork after lining the tins, this allows the air to escape. Bake in a quick oven. Make a cream sauce of one cup of cream, one tablespoonful of butter, and one of flour; season with pepper and salt. Bring the cream to a boil, add the flour which has been made smooth with a little cold milk or water, then the butter, pepper and salt. Put a quart of oysters (no juice) in boiling water until they begin to swell, then drop into the cream sauce. Fill your shells of paste and serve very hot. The puff paste is baked and taken out of the tins before filling.

Miss Hoge.

VEAL PATÉS.

Make a puff paste, roll very thin, and line your pate pans. Mince some cold veal, roll three or four crackers to powder; also chop some cold boiled ham in the proportion of one-third ham to two-thirds veal. Add the cracker to the veal and ham, wet well with gravy and a little milk. If you have no gravy, stir into a cupful of hot milk two tablespoonfuls of butter and a beaten egg. Season well with salt and pepper. Have your pans lined with the puff paste, fill with the mixture, and bake. A little oyster liquid improves the gravy.

Miss Hoge.

RICE CROQUETTES.

One large cupful of cooked rice, half a cupful of milk, one egg, one tablespoonful each of sugar and melted butter, half a teaspoonful of salt, a light grating of nutmeg. Put the milk on to boil, add the rice and seasoning. When it boils, add the egg well beaten. Stir till the egg turns a little; then take off and cool. When cold, shape, and roll in egg and crumbs. Fry in boiling lard.

CANNELON OF BEEF.

Two pounds of the round of beef that has hung for several days, the rind of half a lemon, four sprigs of parsley, one teaspoonful of salt, one-fourth teaspoonful of pepper, quarter of a nutmeg, two tablespoonfuls of melted butter, one raw egg, and one teaspoonful of onion juice. Chop meat, parsley and lemon rind *very* fine; add other ingredients, and mix thoroughly; then add one teaspoonful of lemon juice. Shape into rolls about three inches in diameter and six in length. Roll in buttered paper, and bake thirty minutes, basting with butter and water. Place on a hot plate and serve with tomato sauce.

Mrs. Innes.

BAKED DEVILED CRABS.

For one can of crabs make a dressing of two hard-boiled eggs; rub into the yolks three tablespoonfuls of melted butter, add to this two tablespoonfuls of vinegar, two of made mustard; season with cayenne pepper, salt, and the juice of one lemon. Then add the yolk of a raw egg and the white of the boiled eggs, which has been chopped fine, and the uncooked white, which must be slightly beaten before adding. Mix well through the meat; fill the shells lightly with the mixture, sprinkle the tops with cracker crumbs, pour over a little melted butter. Bake brown.

Miss Hoge.

RISSOLES.

Roll the trimmings from pie crust into a sheet about the sixth of an inch thick. Cut this into cakes with the largest patty cutter. Have any kind of meat or fish prepared as for croquettes. Put a heaping spoonful on each cake. Brush the edges of the paste with beaten egg, then fold and press together. When all are done, dip in beaten egg and fry brown in boiling lard. They should cook about eight minutes. Serve hot.

Miss Hoge.

HOMINY CROQUETTE.

To one cupful and a half cooked of pearl hominy, add two tablespoonfuls of melted butter, and stir hard, moistening by degrees with a cupfull of milk, beating to a light soft paste. Put in a teaspoonful of sugar and a well beaten egg. Roll into oval balls with floured hands, dip in beaten egg, then cracker crumbs, and fry in *hot* lard.

CHICKEN AND HAM PIE.

Boil a chicken in as little water as possible until the meat falls from the bones, pick off the meat and chop it rather fine. Season with pepper, salt, nutmeg and lemon juice, one cupful of cold ham chopped fine. Wet the mould and line with slices of hard-boiled eggs; put in a layer of chicken, then thin layer of ham, another layer of chicken, ham and so on, until mould is filled. Boil down the broth, until a cupful remains, season with pepper, and salt, and a little cayenne. Pour this over the chicken, and it will sink through, forming a jelly around it. Let it stand over night, or all day on the ice. If there is any fear of the jelly not being stiff enough, a little gelatine may be soaked, and added to the cupful of stock. Turn from mould and garnish with lemon or parsley.

Miss Mac Connell.

HAM CROQUETTES.

Chop the ham very fine and season with pepper and mustard. With a little flour in the hand make up small balls. Dip in beaten egg, then roll in bread or cracker crumbs and fry to a light brown in hot lard.

Mrs. Cantwell.

EGGS.

OMLETTE.

Five eggs, four tablespoonfuls of milk, one teaspoonful of salt, one of sugar, a pinch of pepper. Beat the yolks to a cream, add milk, sugar, salt, pepper, a teaspoonful of chopped parsley. Beat whites to a *very* stiff froth. Stir lightly in at the last. Have a lump of butter in a skillet, when smoking hot pour in the eggs. When set in the middle, put the skillet in the oven until the eggs are a light brown. Turn out in a hot plate. Serve at once.

Miss Hoge.

FRIED EGGS.

Have some butter in a skillet, when it smokes drop in the eggs carefully. Fry three minutes; dust with pepper and salt, and transfer to a hot dish.

EGGS IN PAPER CASES.

Make a box out of white letter paper. Take one or two eggs, break into box, add pepper, salt and a little butter. Place box on stove and stir eggs constantly while cooking. When cooked serve in the box in which the eggs were.

Mr. J. S. Robinson.

HAM OR TONGUE OMLETTE.

Beat the yolks of seven eggs to a cream, add a teacupful of milk, a teaspoonful each of sugar and salt, a pinch of pepper. Add lastly the whites. Have ready in a hot frying pan a lump of butter, when it hisses pour in the eggs; sprinkle the top *thickly* with minced ham or tongue. When set in the middle, put in a hot oven, until brown on top, turn out on a hot dish with bottom part up. Serve at once; or it will fall.

Miss Hoge.

FRENCH OMLETTE.

Eight eggs well beaten separately. Add to yolks one teacupful of sweet milk, one tablespoonful of flour, one teaspoonful of baking powder, salt and pepper. Beat together well and then stir in whites. Have ready a skillet with melted butter, rather hot, and pour in mixture. Let brown or cook on bottom, then put in oven five or ten minutes.

MRS. RUSSEL.

POACHED EGGS.

Have boiling water in a skillet, break the eggs in carefully. Boil gently three minutes. Take out with a perforated skimmer, drain, and lay upon slices of buttered toast in a hot dish. Garnish with parsley, dust with pepper and salt.

BREADED EGGS.

Boil hard, and cut in *round* thick slices. Pepper and salt, dip in beaten raw egg, then in fine bread crumbs, or cracker crumbs, and fry in hot butter. Serve with cream sauce.

DEVILED EGGS.

Cut six hard boiled eggs in two. Take out the yolks and mash them fine. Add two tablespoonfuls of butter, one of cream, two or three drops of onion juice, a little grated horseradish, just a dash of cayenne, a teaspoonful of vinegar, salt to taste; mix all thoroughly. Fill the hollowed whites with this and serve on a head of lettuce or celery.

STUFFED EGGS.

Boil the eggs hard and cut in two; remove the yolks, mash fine, adding pepper, salt, melted butter and mustard to taste. Fill the cavities and bind the two pieces together. A little chopped parsley can be added or omit the mustard and add a little chopped chicken, in which case roll in egg and cracker crumbs and fry in hot lard.

SCRAMBLED EGGS.

To each egg one tablespoonful of milk or cream. a dash of salt. Beat the eggs, add the salt and milk. Have some melted butter in a saucepan, and when hot add the mixture. Stir over the fire until it thickens. About two minutes will be sufficient.

PICKLED EGGS.

Boil eggs twenty minutes; shell them and place in crock; pour over them spiced vinegar. Will be fit for use in twenty-four hours. If you use vinegar in which beets have been pickled, it makes the eggs a pretty color, and gives a good flavor.

SOFT BOILED EGGS.

Pour *boiling* water over the eggs and set them at the back of the stove, (covered) where the water will keep just at the boiling point but not boil. In *five* minutes they will be set all through and like jelly. Better than three minutes hard boiling, and more digestible.

FLORENTINE EGGS.

Cook two tablespoonfuls of chopped mushrooms (either canned or fresh) and one chopped onion in two tablespoonfuls of butter for five minutes, add one tablespoonful of flour and stir well, then add gradually one cupful of white stock or hot milk, season with one-half teaspoonful of salt, one-fourth saltspoonful of cayenne. Take six hard boiled eggs, separate the yolks and whites. into rings, then chop the other half until very fine. Cut the yolks into quarters. Mix yolks and chopped whites with sauce, turn out on a plate, and garnish with the rings of eggs and sprigs of parsley. A nice dish for breakfast or tea.

Miss Dodge.

SALADS.

MAYONNAISE.

A tablespoonful of mustard, one of sugar, one-tenth of a teaspoonful of cayenne pepper, one teaspoonful of salt, the yolks of three uncooked eggs, the juice of half a lemon, a quarter of a cupful of vinegar, a pint of oil and a cupful of whipped cream. Beat the yolks and dry ingredients until they are very light and thick, with either a spoon or Dover beater. The bowl in which the dressing is made should be set in a pan of ice water during the beating. Add a few drops of oil at a time until the dressing is very *thick* and rather hard, you can then pour in the oil more rapidly. When it getss o thick that the beater turns hard, add a little vinegar; after all the oil and vinegar have been used, add juice of lemon and whipped cream, place on ice until ready for use. The cream may be omitted if one wishes.

CELERY SALAD.

Let the celery stand in ice water twenty minutes and shake dry. Always cut celery cross-wise in pieces three-fourths of an inch long; if very thick celery, cut in smaller pieces, it is then ready for chicken and celery salad.

Mrs. Innes.

CHICKEN SALAD.

Boil a chicken until tender. When cold separate the meat from the bones; cut into medium sized blocks, *do not mince*. Prepare celery as in previous directions. Take equal quantities of celery and chicken, sprinkle the chicken slightly with salt and pepper; then pour on the Mayonnaise dressing mixing thoroughly with a fork.

Do not let salad stand over two hours after mixing.

A rich salad like chicken salad is too heavy for formal dinners.

Lettuce with French dressing is the best salad to use.

Mrs. Innes.

SALAD DRESSING.

The yolks of two hard boiled eggs, one teaspoonful each of pepper and salt, one tablespoonful of made mustard, three tablespoonfuls each of salad oil and of melted butter, two tablespoonfuls of white sugar, half a teacupful of vinegar, one raw egg, well beaten, a pinch of cayenne pepper, half a cupful of whipped cream. Rub yolks to a powder, add salt, pepper and sugar, then the oil and butter, grinding hard, and putting in but a few drops at a time. The mustard comes next, let all stand together while you beat the raw egg to a froth. Beat this into the dressing, pour in the vinegar spoonful by spoonful, whipping the dressing well as you do it. Add the whipped cream before the dressing is poured over your meat or fish.

Miss Hoge.

FRENCH DRESSING.

Three tablespoonfuls of oil, one of vinegar, one salt spoonful of salt, one-half a salt spoonful of pepper. Put the salt and pepper into a cup and add one tablespoonful of the oil. When thoroughly mixed, add the remainder of the oil and vinegar. This is dressing sufficient for six persons. Many like grated onion juice in the dressing.

CHICKEN SALAD.

Prepare your chicken and celery as in above receipt; mix with the following dressing,— the yolks of two hard boiled eggs, one teaspoonful each of pepper and salt, one tablespoonful of made mustard, three tablespoonfuls each of salad oil and of melted butter, two tablespoonfuls of white sugar, half a teacupful of vinegar, one raw egg well beaten, and a pinch of cayenne pepper. Just before serving, stir through half a cupful of whipped cream. Rub yolks to a fine powder, add salt, pepper and sugar, then the oil and butter, grinding hard, and putting in but a few drops at a time. The mustard comes next, let all stand together while you beat the raw egg to a froth. Beat this into the dressing and pour in the vinegar spoonful by spoonful, whipping the dressing well as you do it. Sprinkle a little salt and pepper over the meat and celery, toss up lightly with a silver fork; pour the dressing over it, mixing well. Add whipped cream just before serving.

MRS. HOGE.

LETTUCE SALAD.

Break off the leaves from the heads of lettuce, wash and throw into cold water for half an hour, drain and lay upon a cloth to absorb water. Put lettuce into salad bowl and pour over the French dressing, carefully turning the leaves. Do not prepare your lettuce salad until a few moments before serving. The dressing can be made any time. Crackers, cheese and olives are passed with lettuce.

MRS. INNES.

CHEESE SALAD OR MOCK CRAB.

One-half pound of pickled shrimps, one-fourth pound of good old cheese; one tablespoonful of salad oil; one teaspoonful each of cayenne pepper, salt and white sugar, and made mustard, four tablespoonfuls of celery vinegar. Mince the shrimps, and grate the cheese. Stir the various condiments into the cheese, adding vinegar last. Let all stand together ten minutes before adding the shrimps. Garnish with lemon.

LOBSTER SALAD.

Cut up and season lobster as you would chicken; use either celery or lettuce, if lettuce, take little crisp leaves, wash and lay them in ice water for a few moments, then put on ice. Take the leaves and make sheets and place salad in them with a tablespoonful of salad dressing on lobster. The little pieces of celery would be used as a garnish. Mayonnaise dressing can be used in place of salad dressing.

SHRIMP SALAD.

To each person serve four shrimps on a lettuce leaf and pour Mayonnaise dressing over the shrimps.

TOMATO SALAD.

Pare smooth, ripe tomatoes; if large cut in half; if not simply remove the core, and fill the space with Mayonnaise. Serve on lettuce leaves.

Garden cress, radishes, beet-root, pepper grass, water cress, cauliflower and cucumbers can be used for salad.

Miss Hoge.

POTATO SALAD,—PLAIN.

One dozen small boiled potatoes sliced thin, chop one onion and put with potatoes; add pepper and salt to taste, and one half cupful of boiling water. Heat one half teacupful of vinegar with two tablespoonfuls of olive oil and pour over potatoes.

Miss Robinson.

POTATO SALAD.

Cut six medium sized cold boiled potatoes in the form of dice, grate one small onion and pour over one half teacupful of boiling water; then add Mayonnaise dressing. Three finely cut stalks of celery are an improvement and some add a little parsley.

Miss Robinson.

CABBAGE SALAD.

To one quart of cut cabbage, one teaspoonful of salt, one-half teaspoonful of pepper, two teaspoonfuls of sugar, one teaspoonful of mustard; add hot dressing as follows, two eggs well beaten, three-fourths of a cupful of vinegar, butter size of a walnut; put on stove and cook until thick. Pour over cabbage and beat until light. Put out to cool and just before serving add one-half pint of cream whipped.

Miss Robinson.

ORANGE SALAD.

Remove skin from oranges and separate the orange into sections, tearing each section into little pieces. Serve with French dressing, leaving out onion juice. This is nice with meats and game.

Mrs. Mac Connell.

AN EASY MAYONNAISE.

Into a small saucepan clean and bright, break the yolk of one egg, one teaspoonful of dry mustard, one salt-spoonful of salt, one-half salt-spoonful of cayenne pepper, three tablespoonfuls of rich, sweet cream, one tablespoonful of cider vinegar. Stir these ingredients together until smooth, then set your saucepan into a vessel of boiling water on the stove, stirring the mixture all the time. In a few minutes it will begin to thicken; when it is as thick as butter, take from the stove and set away to cool; when quite cool, you can stir in as much oil as you like; it will take a surprising quantity, and is quicker made and much more likely to give satisfaction than the old way of adding a drop at a time.

Miss M. W. Cumming.

LOBSTER SALAD.

French dressing which must be first poured over the lobster,— called marinating it. Use French dressing after receipt given. Mayonnaise dressing made as follows,— mix one teaspoonful of dry mustard, one teaspoonful of sugar, one-half teaspoonful of salt, one-fourth salt-spoonful of cayenne pepper, then add yolks of two raw eggs, and stir well. Stir in slowly one pint of olive oil, adding two tablespoonfuls of vinegar or of lemon juice; put together as in Mayonnaise dressing receipt. Cut one pint of lobster meat, fresh, or one can, into dice, season with the French dressing, and keep on ice until ready for use then mix; with it half the Mayonnaise. Make nests or cups of crisp lettuce leaves; break the fuller leaves, and mix with the lobster; put a spoonful of lobster on each cup, with a spoonful of Mayonnaise on top. Garnish with capers and lobster claws when you use fresh lobster.

Miss Dodge.

SALADS.

SWEET-BREAD SALAD.

Boil sweet-breads thoroughly, until they drop easily from a fork. When cold cut into small pieces. A half hour before serving pour over them Mayonnaise dressing and set away in a cool place.

Mrs. Innes.

CELERY SALAD.

Prepare celery as in previous directions. Salt slightly, and pour over it Mayonnaise dressing. Garnish salad bowl with small celery beans.

SALMON SALAD.

One can of salmon with skin and bone removed. Six fresh crackers rolled fine. Mash salmon with a silver fork until very smooth, add crackers and the heart of two heads of celery chopped fine. Mix the juice of three lemons with the meat and add Mayonnaise dressing.

Miss Robinson.

OYSTER SALAD.

One pint of oysters steamed five minutes. When cold cut into not too fine pieces, one pint and a half of celery cut in pieces, one pint of cracker crumbs. Mix well together with rich salad dressing or Mayonnaise.

Miss Hoge.

OYSTER SALAD.

One pint of celery cut in small pieces, one quart of oysters, three tablespoonfuls of vinegar one of oil, half a teaspoonful of salt, one-eighth teaspoonful of pepper, two tablespoonfuls of lemon juice; let oysters come to a boil in their own liquor. Skim well and drain. Season them with oil, salt, pepper, lemon juice and vinegar. When *cold* and ready to serve, add celery which has been on ice, and one-half cupful of Mayonnaise dressing. One half of the dressing to be mixed with oysters and celery, and the rest used with celery leaves to garnish. The salad dressing after whipped cream has been added, can be used and is very nice.

Miss Robinson.

SANDWICHES.

HAM SANDWICHES.

Cut some fresh bread in thin slices (cutting off crust) and butter. Cut some cold boiled ham very fine, also a few little cucumber pickles. Mix until moist with salad dressing, adding more mustard if you wish. Spread between slices of bread. The bread can be cut in large squares, spread with mixture and roll, pinching each roll at the end to keep it in shape, or tie each sandwich with a ribbon.

STUFFED ROLLS.

Cut off the end of a roll and remove the inside, leaving only the crust. Fill with a mixture of cheese, ham or chicken sandwiches, covering top with the small slice cut off. This is nice for picnics, or a lunch for traveling.

CHICKEN AND VEAL SANDWICHES.

Take equal parts of cold chopped chicken and veal with a little chopped pickle. Mix with Mayonnaise dressing and spread thin slices of buttered bread with mixture, and fit another slice of bread on top. The secret of nice sandwiches is in having the bread fresh, cut thin, and the meat well seasoned.

CHEESE SANDWICHES.

Take rich cheese and mash with silver fork, say one-fourth pound of cheese, yolks, of two hard boiled eggs mixed with cheese; add enough Mayonnaise dressing to season well. Cut the bread in thin slices and butter, spreading cheese between slices. A leaf of lettuce can be placed with the cheese between bread. These sandwiches are nice served with salad.

VEGETABLES.

All green vegetables must be washed thoroughly in cold water before cooking. There should be a tablespoonful of salt for every two quarts of water. If the water boils a long time before the vegetables are put in, it loses all its gases and the vegetables will not have a fine flavor. The time for boiling green vegetables depends very much upon the age, and how long they have been gathered.

The following is a time-table for cooking:

Potatoes, boiled	30 minutes.
Potatoes, baked	45 minutes.
Sweet potatoes, boiled	45 minutes.
Sweet potatoes, baked	1 hour.
Squash, boiled	25 minutes.
Squash, baked	45 minutes.
Green peas, boiled	20 to 40 minutes.
Shell beans, boiled	1 hour.
String beans, boiled	1 to 2 hours.
Green corn	25 minutes to 1 hour.
Asparagus	15 to 30 minutes.
Spinach	15 minutes.
Tomatoes, fresh	1 hour.
Tomatoes, canned	30 minutes.
Cabbage	45 minutes to 2 hours.
Cauliflower	1 to 2 hours.
Beet greens	1 hour.
Onions	1 to 2 hours.
Beets	1 to 5 hours.
Turnips, white	45 minutes to 1 hour.
Turnips, yellow	1½ to 2 hours.
Parsnips	1 to 2 hours.
Carrots	1 to 2 hours.

BOILED POTATOES.

Twelve medium sized potatoes, one tablespoonful of salt, boiling water to cover. Pare the potatoes, and if old, let them stand in water an hour or two to freshen them. Boil fifteen minutes; then add the salt, and boil fifteen minutes longer. Pour off every drop of water; take the cover from the saucepan, and shake the potatoes in a current of cold air (at either door or window). Place the saucepan in the back of the stove, and cover until serving time. The sooner the potatoes are served the better.

Mrs. W. S. Robinson.

MASHED POTATOES.

Twelve potatoes, pare and boil as for boiled potatoes, and mash fine and light. Add one tablespoonful of salt and one of butter. Beat well; then add half a cup of boiling milk, and beat as you would for cake. This will give a light and delicate dish of potatoes. The potatoes must be perfectly smooth before adding the other ingredients.

SCALLOPED POTATOES.

Put a little butter in a baking-dish, then a layer of raw potatoes sliced thin, salt, pepper and bits of butter; then another layer of potatoes and seasoning, till the dish is full. Fill half or two-thirds full of sweet milk or cream, sprinkle bread-crumbs over the top and bake an hour.

Mrs. Spelman.

SARATOGA POTATOES.

Select two or three large potatoes and cut in *thin* slices on the cabbage cutter. These are placed for half an hour in ice water; see that the boiling lard in which they are to be fried, is of the proper temperature; fry quickly a light brown, sprinkle with salt, and put into a pan on a coarse cloth to absorb the grease. Do not fry too many at a time. The potatoes may be cooked early in the day, and can be warmed or eaten cold.

BOILED SWEET POTATOES.

Have them all as nearly the same size as possible; put into cold water without any salt, and boil until a fork will easily pierce the largest. Turn off the water, and lay them in the oven to dry for five minutes. Peel before sending to the table. Or *parboil*, then peel and roast or fry.

Mrs. W. S. Robinson.

JERSEY SWEET POTATOES.

Boil until tender, peel, slice lengthwise, sprinkle with granulated sugar, pour melted butter over them, and put in the oven to brown. Baste with butter a second time if they look dry.

Miss Hoge.

MINCED POTATOES.

Boil potatoes with the skins on until almost done. When cold peel, cut in pieces the size of dice. season with cayenne pepper, salt, and parsley. Have a frying pan with some *hot* butter in it; pour in the potatoes, press together, cover tightly and cook ten to fifteen minutes. Turn out on hot dish with crust up

Miss Hoge.

POTATOES WITH STOCK.

One quart of cold boiled potatoes cut into dice, one pint of stock a little minced parsley, one tablespoonful of butter, a little lemon juice, salt, pepper, and a little onion. Season the potatoes with pepper and salt, add stock and let cook ten minutes; then add lemon, parsley, and onion, cook three minutes and serve.

POTATO PUFF.

Stir two cup cupfuls of mashed potatoes, two tablespoonfuls of melted butter, and some salt to a fine and creamy condition; then add two eggs, well beaten separately, and six tablespoonfuls of cream, beat it all well and lightly together, pile in the dish, and grate cheese over the top; bake in a quick oven until a delicate brown.

ESCALOPED POTATOES.

Cut one quart of cold boiled potatoes in *very thin* slices and season well with pepper and salt. Butter a pudding-dish, cover the bottom with a layer of cream sauce, add a layer of potatoes, sprinkle with chopped parsley, and moisten with sauce. Continue this until all the material is used. Have the last layer of the sauce; cover the dish with fine bread crumbs, grated cheese, and small bits of butter; cook twenty minutes. This receipt takes one pint of the cream sauce, one tablespoonful of parsley, half a cupful of bread, crumbs, pepper and salt to taste.

Mrs. Innes.

RICED POTATOES.

Press mashed potatoes through a colander, or Henis fruit press, into the dish in which they are to be served. Have both dish and colander hot; the potatoes resemble rice. Be careful not to press the potatoes after they are in the dish; serve hot.

MASHED SWEET POTATOES.

Take twelve medium sized potatoes, boil until tender. Peel, and mash like Irish potatoes; add salt, pepper and *three* tablespoonfuls of *hot* cream or milk; beat thoroughly. Pile in a baking dish, smooth over, make a hole in the top with a spoon, and fill with butter. Set in the oven and brown quickly.

Mrs. J Powell.

ASPARAGUS.

Put the stalks into bundles, cut them the same length, tie up with cord, and boil in hot water without salt for twenty-five minutes; remove the strings and serve on buttered toast, pour over some melted butter, and season with pepper and salt. A poached egg is nice to serve in each slice of the toast and asparagus. The stalks must be scraped below the green head before boiling, and keep in cold water until ready to cook.

Mrs. W. S. Robinson.

STEWED CAULIFLOWER.

Select nice heades of cauliflower, lay in salt water for half an hour if not perfectly fresh. Then tie the heads in netting and stew in boiling water half an hour, or until tender. Remove the netting, place in a hot dish and serve with melted butter or *cream sauce* It is nice to serve the sauce in a sauce boat.

Miss Hoge.

GREEN PEAS.

Pick, shell, and wash, put them into boiling water previously salted; when tender take them up in a little of the liquor in which they were boiled; butter and pepper them. Some prefer a little sweet cream. If they are cooked immediately upon gathering, they will need no sugar, if allowed to remain twelve hours or more a tablespoonful of sugar will be found an addition. A sprig of mint or three or four green pea shells may be added while boiling.

FRIED APPLES.

Pare and slice one quart of apples. Put butter into frying pan and let get smoking hot, then put in apples with one teacupful of sugar, and let cook slowly for half an hour. A little ground cinnamon can be sprinkled over them.

BAKED APPLES.

Take tart apples; cut out the stem, and flower end also, but do not pare them; wash and place them in a pie dish; fill the cavities with sugar, sprinkle some over them and put pieces of butter on each apple. Pour a little boiling water in the dish and bake until done.

APPLE SAUCE.

Pare, core and slice tart apples, just cover with boiling water and stew until tender. Mash fine, sweeten to taste, add a small piece of butter; season with nutmeg or cinnamon. Beat well together, and cook ten minutes more.

BAKED APPLES.

Take tart apples, pare and cut in halves, sprinkle sugar, cinnamon, and little pieces of butter on each half, and bake until done. Serve with cream.

CINNAMON APPLE SAUCE.

Make a rich syrup; and add to it some stick cinnamon. Have the the apples pared and cut into quarters, drop into the syrup, and cook until clear. Pour into a glass dish.

Mrs. Robinson.

STEWED TOMATOES.

Peel and cut tomatoes into small pieces; stew until tender; season with pepper, salt, butter, a handful of bread-crumbs, a tablespoonful of sugar, a little flour wet with cold cream and a teacupful of cream. A little chopped onion is quite an improvement.

Miss Hoge.

SCALLOPED TOMATOES.

One pint of fresh or canned tomatoes, one large pint of bread-crumbs, four small tablespoonfuls of butter, two tablespoonfuls of sugar, salt and pepper to taste. Put a layer of tomatoes into a baking-dish, dredge with salt, pepper and little pieces of butter, then cover with bread-crumbs; add more tomatoes, pepper, salt, butter and crumbs, until all the ingredients are used; crumbs and little pieces of butter should come last. When fresh tomatoes are used, bake an hour; but for canned tomatoes, one-half an hour.

BROILED TOMATOES.

Cut the tomatoes in thin slices; sprinkle each slice with bread-crumbs, pepper and salt, broil eight minutes, put into a hot dish, and place in the oven for a few minutes. Small pieces of butter should be put on each slice. A little sugar on each slice may be added.

BAKED TOMATOES.

Take eight or ten large, fine, ripe tomatoes; skin and cut out the core. Place in a baking pan, and fill the centers with butter; sprinkle with pepper and sugar. Dredge over with flour; pour small teacupful of cold water in the pan. Bake half an hour in a moderate oven.

MISS A. POWELL.

MOCK OYSTERS OF CORN.

Take a dozen and a half ears of young corn; grate all the grains off as fine as possible. Mix with the grated corn three tablespoonfuls of flour and the yolks of six eggs, well beaten; beat *hard*. Have ready in a frying-pan, a tablespoonful of butter; when hot drop in portions of the mixture about the size of an oyster. They should be quite thick and a light brown.

MRS. W. S. ROBINSON.

GREEN CORN PUDDING.

To one dozen ears of grated corn, add the beaten yolks of five eggs, stir hard, then add two tablespoonfuls of melted butter, one and a half pints of milk, add milk gradually, stirring all the time, then one tablespoonful of sugar, and a little salt; lastly the whites of the eggs which have been beaten to a stiff froth. Bake slowly at first, covering the dish, for an hour. Remove cover, and brown.

MISS HOGE.

SUCCOTASH.

This is made of green corn and Lima beans or butter beans. Have a third more corn than beans when the former has been cut from the cob and the beans shelled. Boil the beans in water until about half done; drain, add the corn, and a cupful of cream or milk, a lump of butter, a teaspoonful of flour wet with a little cold milk; pepper and salt to taste. Cook about twenty minutes after the corn is in.

FRIED CORN.

Cut the corn from the cob and scrape out all the milk. Have ready in a frying-pan a little melted butter; when very hot add the corn, cover, and fry for fifteen minutes. When it begins to brown, sprinkle with a little salt and pepper. Stir often.

STEWED GREEN CORN.

Cut from the cob, and stew fifteen minutes in boiling water. Turn off the water, cover with cold milk, and stew until tender, then add a lump of butter, a little flour wet with cold milk; season with pepper and salt. Boil five minutes, and serve.

CORN OYSTERS.

To one pint of grated corn, add one scant half cupful of melted butter, three tablespoonfuls of milk, two teaspoonfuls of salt, and one-fourth teaspoonful of pepper; beat well for five minutes. Have butter very hot in a frying-pan, drop batter from a spoon, and fry until brown on both sides.

Mrs. Modisette.

CORN FRITTERS.

Six ears of grated corn, one egg, one tablespoonful of flour or rolled cracker, pepper and salt to taste. Fry in hot butter.

GREEN CORN.

Boil the corn on the ear; cut off, and dress with butter, pepper and salt; put into a dish in the oven, five minutes before serving.

LIMA AND BUTTER BEANS.

Shell into cold water; let them stand awhile. Put into a pot with plenty of boiling water and a little salt; cook fast until tender. Large beans sometimes require nearly an hour's boiling; average time is forty minutes. Drain, season with pepper and salt; pour melted butter or cream dressing over the beans.

OKRA.

Boil the pods in salted water until tender. Drain thoroughly; season with pepper and salt to taste. Pour melted butter over them before serving.

Miss Hoge.

SPINACH.

Pick over, wash, and cut off the root; boil in salted water twenty minutes, drain and press through a colander, or chop. For a peck of spinach, add one tablespoonful of butter, two of cream, salt and pepper to taste. Lay slices of hard boiled eggs around it.

CARROTS.

Scrape, and boil from half an hour to an hour. When tender, drain and cut into slices a quarter of an inch thick; then make a butter sauce, and pour over them; or they may be fried with a little butter. Young carrots two inches long, are excellent fried. They do not need a previous boiling when young.

CREAMED TURNIPS SALAD.

Slice six turnips rather thin, boil until tender in salt water, drain water off and pour over the turnips a pint of cream and thicken with a tablespoonful of flour, rubbed smooth with a little milk; add pepper, two tablespoonfuls of butter, and just before taking from the stove, add half a teacupful of vinegar.

Mrs. Russel.

CREAMED CABBAGE.

Slice fine, half a head of cabbage on a slaw cutter; boil until tender and the water has boiled off, dress with salt, pepper and a pint of cream thickened with one tablespoonful of flour rubbed smooth. Let cook a few moments, and if you wish, just before taking from the stove, add half a teacupful of vinegar.

STEAMED CELERY.

Scrape the stocks and cut into pieces an inch long. Boil in salted water until tender. Drain and pour over them a cream sauce, let all boil up together a few minutes.

PARSNIPS.

Scrape and split them, and put into a pot of boiling water; cook until tender; dress with plenty of butter, salt and pepper. Or you may parboil them and dip into beaten eggs and grated crackers, and fry in hot lard.

SALSIFY OR OYSTER PLANT.

Scrape the roots, cut into two inch pieces or smaller, and lay in cold water to keep from turning black. Boil in salted water from half an hour to an hour, according to size of root. Make a cream sauce and when boiling drain the roots and simmer gently for ten minutes. Salsify is rather tasteless until after frost.

Mrs. W. S. Robinson.

BOILED BEETS.

Boil the beets until tender, with the skins on; then take out and put for a minute in a pan of cold water; rub off the skin and slice into a vegetable dish; salt and pepper them, and pour over them a tablespoonful of melted butter.

BOILED ONIONS.

Put in salted boiling water and cook until tender, pour off the water and cover with a white sauce. Let them simmer a few minutes.

BAKED ONIONS.

Parboil large onions, and when they begin to look clear, drain them and set in a baking pan, cover with a cream sauce, sprinkle with bread crumbs and bake twenty minutes.

STUFFED ONIONS.

Parboil and cut out the heart of the onions. Fill with any kind of meat finely chopped and highly seasoned. When the onions are filled put a bit of butter on each. Cover with bread crumbs and bake one hour. Serve with cream sauce.

FRIED EGG PLANT.

Cut the plant in slices about one-third of an inch thick. Pare and lay in a deep dish; cover with salted water and let stand one hour. Drain and pepper the slices slightly, and dip in beaten egg and bread crumbs. Fry in boiling fat for ten minutes. Or they can be fried in just enough butter to brown them.

STUFFED EGG PLANT.

Parboil for ten minutes. Slit down the side, and extract the seeds. Prop open the slit with a bit of clean wood, and lay in cold salt and water. Make a stuffing of bread crumbs, minute pieces of fat pork, salt, pepper, nutmeg, parsley, and a *little* chopped onion. Moisten with cream, and bind with a beaten egg. Fill the egg plants, wind soft thread about them to keep the slit shut; put into a dripping pan with a little water and bake. Baste with butter and water. Test with a straw to see they are tender. Lay the egg plant in a dish, add to the gravy three tablespoonfuls of cream, thicken with a little flour, put in a teaspoonful of chopped parsley, boil up once, and pour over the egg plants.

RICE.

Wash carefully in cold water. Put into plenty of boiling water slightly salted. Boil hard until the rice is done, but not soft. *Drain perfectly dry*, and cover tight. Set on a double boiler where the rice will *dry out*, but not cook. Take out with a fork, each grain must be separate. To be eaten with roast beef.

Miss Hoge.

STEWED MUSHROOMS.

Take a pint of mushrooms; cut off the stalks, and peel the top skin with a silver knife; put into a saucepan and cover with cold water; stew gently fifteen or twenty minutes. Salt to taste, add a tablespoonful of butter cut into bits and rolled well in flour. Boil five minutes; stir in three tablespoonfuls of cream. A beaten egg also is an improvement, but care must be taken that it does not curdle. Serve on toast. All stirring should be done with a silver spoon; if it turns black, they are not mushrooms, and should be thrown away.

BAKED BEANS.

Mash the beans in warm water. Put in pot with plenty of *hard* water, and let simmer until they are transparent; or begin to sink, then throw in colander to drain. Put back in pot and pour on boiling water and let come to a boil. Place half the beans in the bottom of a gallon crock, and in the center a nice piece of uncooked pork seasoned with pepper, cover with the rest of the beans within three inches of the top of crock and pour boiling water until you can see it between the beans. Cover with a plate and bake six hours in a slow oven. Whenever the water has cooked down so you cannot see it, pour on more boiling water. If, when you taste them, they are not seasoned enough, put a little salt in a cup and pour boiling water on it and pour over beans. The last water should not be poured on, over half an hour before the beans are done. A tablespoonful of molasses can be added.

Mrs. Russell.

PEARL HOMINY.

Wash a cupful of hominy in cold water; then stir it into one quart of boiling water, with a teaspoonful of salt, boil about thirty minutes. Stir several times. Be careful that the hominy does not burn.

BREADS.

YEAST.

One quart of pared potatoes, two quarts of water, one small pint of hops, tied in a thin muslin bag, and boil with potatoes. Take one tablespoonful of flour, and put in crock and scald with potato water. Mash potatoes and add to flour. Add one small teacupful of brown sugar, one tablespoonful of ginger, and one tablespoonful of salt. If when all together, it does not make two quarts, add enough cold water to make that quantity. While lukewarm add one-half pint of yeast.

Mrs. Robinson.

POTATO YEAST.

Six large potatoes grated raw, one teacupful of flour, one teacupful of sugar, one-half teacupful of salt, one small tablespoonful of ginger. Small handful of hops boiled in two quarts of water down to one quart. Pour hop water over the other ingredients hot and stir until it thickens when cold, add a small quantity of yeast.

Mrs. Spelman.

BREAD.

Take one pint of potatoes and boil in three pints of water; when potatoes are cooked, scald a small teacupful of flour with the potato water; mash potatoes and add. If the water has boiled away add enough lukewarm water to potatoes and flour to make two quarts; thicken with flour, and add small teacupful of yeast. Let rise over night in a warm place; in the morning add two small tablespoonfuls of salt, one tablespoonful of sugar, one tablespoonful of lard, and flour enough to knead well. Let rise and when light roll into loaves and put into pans. Let rise until light, then bake from three-quarters to one hour. This will make three loaves.

BREAD.

Peel three medium sized potatoes, boil in one quart of water. Put a teacupful of flour into a gallon jar, rub the potato through the colander into the flour; then pour the water in which the potatoes were boiled over the mixture, and be sure the water is hot enough to scald the flour thoroughly. Then add water until jar is about half full, keep blood heat, thicken with flour, make a tolerably stiff batter, put in one cake of good yeast, dissolved in warm water, or a teacupful of home-made yeast, set to rise in a moderately warm place; in the morning it will be to the top of the jar, possibly over. Sift into a bread-bowl four or five quarts of flour, make a space in center, put in a small handful of salt, then beat sponge for five minutes, pour into flour and mix. Right here is the place to be very careful. If your flour is of the very best brands, mix in lightly and smoothly, only enough to make a moist dough. Set to rise where it will be warm, not hot. When light mold into five or six loaves; use only flour enough to keep from sticking to the board; knead five or ten minutes. The poorer or cheap brands of flour sometimes run and become watery in the process of rising; in this case use more flour.

Mrs. Day.

BROWN BREAD.

One pint of Graham flour, one pint of wheat flour; mix well together, and add one pint of yeast sponge, one-half cupful of sugar, lard the size of an egg, one teaspoonful of salt and one-half pint of warm water. Mix it as quickly and softly as possible. Let rise and when light knead quickly and put in pans. When light bake.

Mrs. Robinson.

BOSTON BROWN BREAD.

Three cups white corn meal, two cups graham flour, one cup molasses, one quart milk and salt. Steam four hours.

Mrs. A Folger.

EASY BREAD.

Two quarts of flour, half a cupful of yeast, half a tablespoonful each of sugar and salt, about a pint and a half of warm water, or milk if preferred. The milk makes a richer, whiter bread, but dries out quickly. Take out a little of the flour for kneading, and beat the other ingredien's well with a spoon. When thoroughly mixed turn out on the board and knead hard for half an hour. Put back in bowl or large pan, rub a little melted lard over the surface, cover closely, and let rise eight or nine hours. In the morning mold into loaves, set in a warm place and let rise an hour. Bake one hour in a moderate oven. These quantities will make two loaves.

Mrs. W. S. Robinson.

SWEET RUSKS.

One quart of bread sponge, two coffee cupfuls of sugar, three-fourths cupful of butter, four eggs, one-fourth of a nutmeg. Beat butter in sponge, eggs and sugar together until very light, then stir all together. Stir in enough flour to make batter thick enough to drop from a spoon. Let rise until light. When light knead fifteen minutes, having dough soft. Let rise again, and and when light turn on bread board and roll an inch thick, cut with biscuit cutter and let rise. Bake in moderate oven fifteen to twenty minutes. When baked have the whites of two eggs beaten to a stiff froth; spread over top of rusks, and sprinkle granulated sugar and ground cinnamon over the egg. Put in oven and let brown. "Practice makes perfect" with these rusks.

Mrs. Gage.

MUSH BISCUIT.

Take a quart of warm mush; have some sifted flour in a pan, put the mush in the center. Work in a tablespoonful each of lard and white sugar, one teaspoonful of salt, half a teaspoonful of soda. Mix with the flour until as stiff as bread dough; let rise, work done, cut with a biscuit cutter; let rise the second time, then bake brown.

Mrs. Hoge.

LIGHT ROLLS.

Two quarts of flour with four tablespoonfuls of lard mixed with one teaspoonful of salt, one tablespoonful of sugar. Make a hole in the middle of the flour, then pour in one pint of cold boiled milk, and one-half cupful of yeast. Fix in the evening, let it stand until morning, then stir until all the flour is thoroughly mixed; let it stand till noon, then lay on a bread board, roll as common biscuit, cut round, grease on the top, then fold over, let rise and bake.

Mrs. Russell.

SWEET MILK WAFFLES.

Two eggs beaten separately, one pint of sweet milk, piece of butter size of an egg, two teaspoonfuls of Royal Baking Powder, one pint and a half of flour, pinch of salt. Beat yolks, add milk, melted butter, flour and baking powder. Just before baking, add beaten whites of eggs. Have your waffle iron well greased and smoking hot.

Mrs. Robinson.

CORN CAKES.

Two eggs beaten separately; to the yellows add one pint of sour milk, one scant teaspoonful of soda, one teaspoonful of salt, corn-meal and flour (three-fourths corn-meal, one-fourth flour) to make a good batter.

Miss Hoge.

BUTTERMILK BISCUIT.

One pint of buttermilk, one teaspoonful of soda, two teaspoonfuls of melted butter, one teaspoonful of sugar, and flour enough to make a very soft dough. Bake in a quick oven.

Mrs. Hoge.

WAFFLES.

Beat three eggs separately, to the yolks add one pint of sour milk, one scant teaspoonful of soda, and tablespoonful of melted butter, one teaspoonful of salt, a heaping pint of flour.

Miss Hoge.

CORN-BREAD.

Rub one teaspoonful of soda through two cupfuls of corn-meal and one cupful of flour, one tablespoonful of sugar, one teaspoonful of salt, two eggs; add buttermilk or sour milk to make a stiff batter. Beat thoroughly, and bake quickly.

Mrs. Fisher.

GRAHAM GEMS.

One cup of sweet milk, one tablespoonful of sugar, one teaspoonful of Royal Baking Powder, pinch of salt, and graham flour sufficient to make a moderately stiff batter.

Miss Low.

GRAHAM MUFFINS.

One quart of graham flour, one-half cup of brown sugar, one teaspoonful of salt, two tablespoonfuls of yeast, add warm milk so that you can stir readily with a spoon; let rise, when light stir again and drop into rings and bake.

Miss Hoge.

FLANNEL CAKES.

Beat two eggs sparately, to the yellows add one pint of sour or buttermilk (if very sour add a little sweet milk), one scant teaspoonful of soda, flour sufficient to make a thin batter, add beaten whites last, bake in large cakes on a griddle.

Miss Hoge.

WHITE MUFFINS.

Beat two eggs separately, to the yellows add one cup of milk, three cups of flour, to which has been added three teaspoonfuls of Royal Baking Powder, one-fourth cup of sugar, piece of butter size of an egg, stir quickly, then add the beaten whites; bake quickly in well greased muffin pans.

Mrs. Hedges.

CAMP MEETING CAKES.

Two eggs, two cups of flour, one cup of sweet milk, one cup of corn meal, one-half cup of butter, one-fourth cup of sugar, add three teaspoonfuls of Royal Baking Powder to the flour; bake in muffin tins.
MRS. HEDGES.

BAKING POWDER BISCUIT.

Sift through one quart of flour, four teaspoonfuls of Royal Baking Powder and one scant teaspoonful of salt, one small tablespoonful of lard; add enough milk to make a soft dough.
MISS HOGE.

SALLY LUNN.

Beat two eggs separately, to the yolks add one cupful of milk, one heaping teaspoonful of sugar, one scant teaspoonful of salt, one pint of flour, one teaspoonful of Royal Baking Powder, one-fourth cupful of melted butter and lard, then the whites; pour in a buttered pan, bake in a hot oven thirty minutes.
MISS HOGE.

SCOTCH SHORT BREAD.

One-half pound of butter, rub in one pound of flour, four ounces of white sugar—rub and beat with hand until it becomes a smooth nice dough; pat in flat pan, bake in moderate oven for half an hour.
MISS MATTHEWS.

SALLY LUNN.

One cup sugar, one cup butter, one cup cream, one cup yeast, six eggs, wine glass brandy, wine glass rose water, sufficient flour for stiff batter: set eight hours before baking, let rise slowly, bake three-fourths of an hour.
MISS MATTHEWS.

CORN BREAD.

One pint buttermilk, one egg beaten up in buttermilk, one and a half pints (scant) of corn meal, mix with it one tablespoonful of sugar, one teaspoonful of soda, one-third teaspoonful of salt; when all are well beaten together stir in one large spoonful of melted lard and bake at once.

Miss Spelman.

ENGLISH MUFFINS.

One quart of flour, one teaspoonful of salt, one-third of a cake of compressed yeast, or one-third of a cupful of liquid yeast one and a half cupfuls of water—have the water blood warm; dissolve the yeast in one-third of a cupful of cold water, add it and the salt to the warm water and gradually stir into the flour; beat the dough thoroughly, cover, and let it rise in a warm place until it is spongy, (rise over night if for breakfast). Sprinkle the breadboard with flour, shape the dough into balls about twice the size of an egg and drop on a greased pan, set on the back part of the stove where there is not much heat; when the cakes have risen a little bake about twenty minutes, tear them apart, butter them and serve.

Mrs. Innes.

GRAHAM GEMS.

One pint of graham flour, one pint of white flour, one pint of milk, one-half cupful of butter, one-half cupful of sugar, two teaspoonfuls of Royal Baking Powder. Be sure and have a quick oven.

Miss Hoge.

DROP BISCUIT.

Ten tablespoonfuls of sifted flour, one teaspoonful of salt, two teaspoonfuls of Royal Baking Powder, two teaspoonfuls of lard or butter; mix salt, baking powder and lard in the flour with a spoon, then stir in milk until you have a stiff batter, drop on gem pans and bake in a quick oven.

Mrs. Binckley.

QUICK BISCUIT.

Mix one teaspoonful of salt into three pints of flour, put one teacupful of milk with two tablespoonfuls of lard on the fire to warm; pour this on two eggs well beaten, add the flour with one cupful of home-made yeast; when well mixed set in a warm place for about four hours to rise, then form into biscuit, then let rise two hours more, then bake.

MARYLAND BISCUIT.

Mix one tablespoonful of butter and one teaspoonful of salt into one quart of flour, work in milk enough to make a stiff dough, beat the dough with a mallet or potato masher five hundred times.

Miss Hoge.

MARYLAND BISCUIT.

One quart of flour (measured before sifting), two tablespoonfuls of lard, one teaspoonful of salt; mix flour and lard thoroughly with hand, then use *ice cold* milk and water to make into a dry stiff dough, so as to merely hold together, dredge the board occasionally with small quantity of flour, knead hard for one hour by hand or beat with ax on biscuit block for half an hour. The dough will become smooth as satin, and blister. Roll out an inch thick, cut, prick the tops and bake at once for half an hour in a moderately hot oven.

Mrs. Garretson.

BUCKWHEAT CAKES.

One quart of buckwheat flour, four tablespoonfuls of yeast, one teaspoonful of salt, one tablespoonful of sugar warm water and milk enough to make a thin batter, beat well and let it stand over night—if the batter is the least sour in the morning stir in a pinch of soda dissolved in hot water. Mix your buckwheat in an earthen crock and leave some each morning to serve as a sponge for the next night instead of using fresh yeast, you add the usual supply of flour, etc., every night. In cold weather this can be done for a week or ten days, then start fresh again.

Miss Hoge.

BUCKWHEAT CAKES.

Scald two gills of Indian meal in one quart of boiling water, add a little salt, when cool add one gill of yeast, and stir in enough buckwheat flour to make a thin batter, let it rise over night; if it should be a little sour in the morning, add one-fourth teaspoonful of soda dissolved in hot water.

SOUTH CAROLINA CORN PONE.

Scald one pint of corn meal with boiling water, add one teaspoonful of salt, one of sugar, one tablespoonful of butter, mould with the hands into oblong cakes, lay in a well greased pan and bake quickly. It should be broken, not cut, and eaten very hot.

Miss Hoge.

BREAD GRIDDLE-CAKES.

One quart of milk, two cups of stale bread crumbs, one-half cup of flour, one tablespoonful of melted butter, three eggs beaten separately, one teaspoonful of salt; work bread and milk smooth, stir in butter and eggs, lastly flour enough to bind the mixture, one teaspoonful of Royal Baking Powder; bake on a griddle.

RICE GRIDDLE-CAKES.

One cup of cold boiled rice, one pint of flour, one teaspoonful of salt, two eggs beaten separately, one scant teaspoonful of soda, enough sour milk to make a batter. Cold hominy can be used in the same way.

PIKELETS OR RAISED PANCAKES.

One pint of milk, one and a half pints of flour, one-half cupful of yeast, two eggs, two tablespoonfuls of melted butter, one teaspoonful of salt, mix milk and flour and add yeast; let rise over night; in the morning add yolks of eggs, melted butter, salt and beaten whites of eggs.

Mrs. Robinson.

GRAHAM GEMS.

Two cups of sugar, one-half cup of butter, three eggs well beaten, one pint of buttermilk, one teaspoonful of soda, add graham flour enough to make stiff as cake dough; bake in gem pans.

Mrs. Janes.

SHORT CAKE.

One pint of flour, butter the size of an egg rubbed through the flour, one teaspoonful of salt, small teacupful of sugar, two teaspoonfuls of Royal Baking Powder, moisten with sweet milk to make a soft dough. It can be rolled thick and split when baked, or baked in two layers; the strawberries can be sweetened and mashed before using or put in the short cake whole with powdered sugar sprinkled over berries, another layer of cake, more berries and sugar.

Mrs. Robinson.

RAISED WAFFLES.

Make as raised pancakes are made, only bake in waffle irons

Mrs Robinson.

CORN MEAL MUSH.

Sprinkle one pint of corn meal into three pints of well salted water and cook three hours, stirring occasionally; keep well covered to prevent crust from forming. Mrs. Henderson gives a receipt for mush as follows: "Put one quart of water on fire to boil, stir a pint of cold milk with one pint of corn meal and one teaspoonful of salt. When the water boils stir in mixture gradually, stirring all well together. Let it boil for half an hour, stirring often to prevent it from burning. Pour in pans and when cold slice and fry in hot lard, or each slice may be dipped in beaten egg, and rolled in bread or cracker-crumbs and fried in hot lard."

Mrs. Robinson.

PIES AND PUDDINGS.

APPLE CREAM PIE.

Line your pie-pan with puff paste; have some apples (three medium apples for one pie) stewed or steamed until tender, place in the pan. Sweeten and flavor with nutmeg, one pint of rich cream; pour over the apples. Bake in a slow oven. The cream will be thick when the pie is cold.

Mrs. Hoge.

APPLE PIE.

Pare, core, and slice tart apples. Line the pie-pan with puff paste, put in a layer of fruit, then sprinkle well with granulated sugar, a little nutmeg or cinnamon, and some small pieces of butter. Do this until the pan is full; cover with a crust and bake. Do not forget to wet the edge of the under crust with cold water before adding the top crust.

Miss Hoge.

RHUBARB PIE.

Skin the stalks, cut in lengths of half an inch; fill the crust with the fruit, strew *thickly* with sugar. Cover with top crust, and bake in a slow oven three-quarters of an hour.

PEACH MERINGUE.

Line your pans with puff paste, fill with canned peaches cut in halves, sweeten to taste; bake fifteen minutes. Make a meringue of whites of eggs and powdered sugar, put a tablespoonful on each half peach, return to oven for a few minutes to brown slightly. Should be eaten the day it is made.

MINCE MEAT.

Two pounds of lean beef, boiled, and when cold, chopped fine, five pounds of apples, pared and chopped; one pound of beef suet, cleared of strings and minced very fine; two pounds of raisins, seeded and chopped; two pounds of currants, washed and *carefully* picked over; three-fourths of a pound of citron, cut up fine; two tablespoonfuls of cinnamon; one tablespoonful each of nutmeg, cloves, allspice and salt; one cup of molasses, two pounds of brown sugar, one quart of sherry, one pint of best French brandy, juice and grated rind of three oranges, enough boiled vinegar to make *very* moist. This mince meat will keep all winter in a cool place. When making your pies add if necessary more liquor and seasoning.

Mrs. Hoge.

CORN MEAL PUDDING.

Eight tablespoonfuls of corn meal boiled in one and a half pints of sweet milk, which makes a mush, three eggs, one cupful of sugar, one-half cupful of molasses, one-half cupful of butter, one tablespoonful of cinnamon, one-half nutmeg, scant teaspoonful of cloves, one fourth teaspoonful of allspice, one heaping teaspoonful of salt, one cupful of seeded raisins add milk enough to make as thin as cream, stir often until it begins to bake. Bake about one and a half hours.

Mrs. Russell.

SWEET POTATO PUDDING.

One pound of boiled sweet potatoes after putting through sieve, one-half pound of sugar, one-half pound of butter, five eggs. Cream the butter and sugar, then add potatoes, slowly beating all the time; add eggs slowly (beaten separately), add the juice and grated rind of two lemons. Bake in pie plates with or without crust.

Miss Matthews.

BATTER PUDDING.

One pint of milk, three eggs, beaten separately; two cupfuls of flour, one teaspoonful of salt, one pinch of soda. Bake in a buttered pudding dish three-quarters of an hour. Serve at once, with a rich sauce.

Miss Hoge.

PLUM PUDDING.

One cup of molasses, one of sugar, one of suet or butter, one of seeded raisins, one of sliced citron, one of currants, one of sweet milk, four and a half of flour, two teaspoonfuls of Royal baking powder. Steam five hours; serve with clear sauce. This pudding can be saved for weeks. Steam enough to heat thoroughly before serving.

Mrs. Philips.

LILLIE'S PUDDING.

One quart of milk heated until boiling, remove from the fire and add gradually the beaten yolks of three eggs and one-half cup of sugar, stir in the beaten whites and heat until it begins to thicken. Have a pudding-dish well buttered, sprinkle the bottom with bread crumbs, pour over these half a cupful of strawberry or other jam; cover this with bread crumbs, then pour on hot mixture carefully. Bake until brown. Eat cold with cream.

Miss Hoge.

QUEEN PUDDING.

One pint of fine bread crumbs; one quart of rich milk, one cup of sugar; yolks of five eggs; grated rind of one lemon; butter size of an egg; one cup of raisins. Bake. Whip the whites of the eggs to a stiff froth, mix in a teacup of sugar, the juice of one lemon. Spread a thin layer of jelly over the top of the pudding then the whites, replace in the oven until a light brown.

Miss Hedges.

RICE MILK.

Three even tablespoonfuls of rice washed, put in pan, add one cupful of sugar, one-fourth nutmeg, and pinch of salt, add to this two quarts of morning milk, bake one hour slowly, add one more quart of milk and bake another hour, stir occasionally during the first hour; one cupful of seeded raisins can be added.

Mrs. Robinson.

APPLE PUDDING.

One and a half pints of apples when pared and steamed, mash through the colander, add scant teacupful of butter while apples are hot, one and a half cupfuls of sugar, one-half nutmeg, three eggs well beaten; make very rich baking powder biscuit dough, and line baking dish; pour in custard and bake until custard is firm.

Mrs. Gage.

STEAMED APPLE PUDDING.

Stew apples until tender, season with sugar, nutmeg and a little butter. Fill a pudding dish two-thirds full with the apples. Make a baking powder dough half an inch thick and cover the dish. Steam from one half to three quarters of an hour. Serve immediately with sugar and cream or a hot sauce.

Mrs. Innes.

SUET PUDDING.

One cup of chopped suet or butter, one cup of molasses, one-half cup of sugar, one-half cup of sour milk, one teaspoonful of soda, one egg, well beaten, one slice of bread crumbled, one-half cup of raisins, one-half cup of currants, one-half teaspoonful of salt; thicken with flour. Pour in a buttered mould and steam three hours. Serve with wine or lemon sauce.

Miss Hoge.

COTTAGE PUDDING.

Rub one cupful of sugar and one tablespoonful of butter to a cream; add the yolks of two eggs, and one cupful of sweet milk. In three cupfuls of flour put two teaspoonfuls of Royal Baking Powder, stir this in, alternating with the beaten whites; flavor with nutmeg. Bake in a buttered mould. Eat with a hot sauce.

Miss Hoge.

CHOCOLATE PUDDING.

One quart of milk, four tablespoonfuls of corn-starch, four and a half of sugar, five of scraped chocolate, and two of boiling water, two eggs, one teaspoonful of salt; reserve one cupful of the milk and put the remainder on to boil, put sugar, chocolate and water in a saucepan and stir over a hot fire for about a minute, when the mixture should be smooth and glossy; stir this into the boiling milk, mix corn starch with the cold milk, beat the eggs and add to the corn starch and milk, add also the salt, stir this into the boiling milk, and beat well about three minutes, turn this into a mould that has been dipped into cold water; serve with cream and and sugar.

Miss Hoge.

RAISIN PUDDING.

Boil two quarts of raisins in one quart of water until soft, add one cup of sugar, make a stiff biscuit dough and cut into small pieces the size of a penny and drop into the fruit while boiling; add one tablespoonful of butter; to make it very rich add half a glassful of currant or other jelly.

Mrs. Falte.

RICE PUDDING.

One quart of rich milk, one small teacupful of rice, one-half cup of sugar, teaspoonful of salt, nutmeg, and a handful of raisins; put rice in a pudding dish, cover with hot water and let it boil until dry, stir in sugar, nutmeg, raisins, one tablespoonful of butter and the milk; bake slowly until rice is done.

Mrs. Hoge.

BROWN BETTY.

One cup of bread crumbs, two cupfuls of chopped apples (tart), one-half cupful of sugar, one teaspoonful of cinnamon, two table spoonfuls of butter cut into small bits; butter a deep dish and put in a layer of the chopped apple at the bottom, sprinkle with sugar, a few bits of butter and cinnamon, cover with bread crumbs, then more apple, proceed in this order until the dish is full, having a layer of crumbs on top, cover closely and steam three-quarters of an hour in a moderate oven, then uncover and brown quickly. Eat warm with sugar and cream, or a sweet sauce.

ORANGE ROLEY-POLEY.

Make a light paste as for apple dumplings, roll in an oblong sheet and lay oranges (sweet ones) peeled, sliced and seeded thickly over it, sprinkle well with white sugar, grate some of the peel over all and roll up closely, folding down the ends to secure the syrup; boil in a pudding cloth, or put in a steamer and steam an hour and a half, serve with lemon sauce. Cherries, applebutter or currants can be used in the same way as oranges; serve them with a sweet sauce.

Miss Hoge.

STEAMED APPLE DUMPLING.

Make a dough of one pint of flour, one teaspoonful of salt, two teaspoonfuls of Royal Baking Powder, half a teacupful of butter, moisten with milk or water; roll as thin as pie crust, wet your cloth with boiling water, sprinkle it with flour, lay in a crock, place the crust on the cloth, fill with sliced apples, pinch the crust together, tie cloth but leave room for swelling; steam two hours.

Mrs. Robinson.

BAKED APPLE DUMPLINGS.

Use the same dough as above, line cups with the dough and fill with the apples, pinch the crust together and bake.

OMLETTE SOUFFLIÉ.

Take a tin or porcelain lined baking dish and butter it thoroughly, put in the bottom to the depth of about an inch any sort of preserves, pineapple, peach, plum, etc., then make an ordinary omlette, substituting for the salt one tablespoonful of sugar, and when beaten properly light pour over the preserves and bake in a quick oven. This is a delicious and easily made dessert, and can be made while the preceding course is being taken from the table.

Miss Cumming.

CABINET PUDDING.

Butter a covered mould and decorate it with candied fruits or raisins which have been seeded, then put in a layer of lady fingers or stale sponge cake, then a little of the fruit, and so on until the mould is nearly full; pour one pint of boiling milk into the yolks of three eggs which have been beaten, with three tablespoonfuls of sugar and one saltspoonful of salt; pour this over the cake in the mould, then steam for one hour and serve with wine or foamy sauce.

Miss Dodge.

APPLE CUSTARD PUDDING.

Pare and grate six large apples, mix with them one-half pint of milk or cream, one tablespoonful of melted butter, one orange, juice and grated rind, one nutmeg grated, and the yolks of two eggs beaten with half a cupful or more of sugar to taste, pour into a buttered pudding dish and bake five to ten minutes in a good oven; meanwhile whip the whites of eggs to a stiff froth and add to it two tablespoonfuls of sugar, for the meringue to cover the pudding. This is best eaten cold with cream, but can be served hot; it is then better without the meringue.

Miss M. W. Cumming.

PASTRY.

Use none but best butter in pastry. A marble slab is a good thing to roll out paste upon; next to this, the best article is a clean board of hard wood; have your butter cold. Make out as squickly as possible. Pastry is always best when fresh. Bake in a moderate oven, and have the heat the same at the top, as at the bottom.

Miss Hoge.

PIE CRUST.

One quart of flour, one-half pound of sweet, firm lard, one-half pound of butter, one small teacupful of ice water, one teaspoonful of salt. Work butter and lard into the flour until it is fine, add salt and the water by degrees.

PUFF PASTE.

One pound of flour, three-quarters of a pound of butter, yolks of two eggs, a little salt, a teaspoonful of sugar, a little very cold (or better, ice-cold) water. Sift and weigh the flour and put it on a board or marble slab, sprinkle a little salt and a very little sugar over it. Beat the yolks of the eggs, and then stir into them a few spoonfuls of ice-cold water; pour this slowly into the center of the flour with the left hand, working it at the same time well into the mass with the tips of the fingers of the right hand. Continue to work it, turning the fingers round and round on the board until you have a well-worked, smooth and firm paste. Work the butter (which should be kept some minutes in very cold water, if it is at all soft) until the moisture and salt are wiped out, and it is quite supple, care must be taken, however, to keep the butter from getting too soft, as in this condition it would ruin the paste. Divide it into three equal parts, spread one part as flatly and evenly as possible over half of the crust, turn the other over half it, folding it a second time from right to left; roll this out, spread the second portion of the butter on half of the crust, fold and roll it out as before, repeating the same process with the third portion of the butter. The paste has now been given what they call three turns; it should be given six turns, turning and rolling paste after butter is in; however after the first three turns, or after the butter is all in, the paste should be placed on the ice, or in a cold place to remain ten or fifteen minutes between each of the last three turns, this will prevent the butter getting soft enough to penetrate the dough. Each time before the dough is folded, it should be turned half round, so as to roll it in a different direction each time, this makes the layers more even. In order to turn the paste, the end may be held to the rolling-pin, then rolling the pin; the dough will fold loosely around it; the board may be sprinkled with flour, then the dough can be unrolled in the side direction; this is better than to turn it with the hands, as it should be handled as little as possible. When folded the last time, put the paste on a platter, cover and place it on the ice for half an hour, or where it may be thoroughly chilled; then roll it out immediately, or so long as it is kept in a half frozen state it may be kept for a day or two. Firm, solid butter should be selected for puff paste. A light crumbling butter would be very unsuitable.

PUFF PASTE.

Rub half a pound of fresh lard into a pound of flour, using just enough very cold water to bind together; roll it out rather thin and spread butter over the surface; then fold the paste, turning it twice. Roll it out again, dredging the board (a marble slab is preferable) with flour; spread on more butter as before and fold it again. The same process is continued a third time, using in all a quarter of a pound of butter, which should at first be divided into three equal parts.

Four cupfuls of sifted flour are a pound; one cupful of lard or butter is a half pound.

MRS. TREAT.

CREAM PIE.

One large pint of cream, one small teacupful of white sugar, three tablespoonfuls of flour rubbed perfectly smooth with cream enough to moisten, one-half nutmeg and a pinch of salt. Bake with lower crust. The whites of two eggs beaten to a froth, can be added to the cream, if the cream is not rich.

Mrs. Gage.

PUMPKIN PIES.

One quart of cream, one pint of stewed pumpkin, six eggs, two cupfuls of sugar, one cupful of molasses, one nutmeg grated, one tablespoonful of ginger, two tablespoonfuls of cinnamon, one small teaspoonful of salt, one tablespoonful of flour, rubbed smooth with a little of the milk. Then stir the flour in the pumpkin, add the sugar, molasses, spices and salt, the eggs thoroughly beaten; the cream last. This quantity will make three pies.

Mrs. Robinson.

APPLE PIE.

Line the sides of a baking dish with pie crust the depth of an inch. Place in the center of dish a small teacup or sauce dish, inverted, fill with tart, ripe apples cut in quarters, sprinkle with sugar, pour in a very little water, add slices of lemon and cover with crust; bake about half an hour.

Miss A. Powell.

MOCK CREAM PIE.

One pint of sweet milk, four tablespoonfuls of sugar, one heaping tablespoonful of flour, rubbed smooth, yolks of two eggs beaten with the flour. Put milk and sugar on stove and let heat, then add eggs, flour a little nutmeg and stir until it thickens. Have the crust in pan, prick and bake; pour in custard. Beat whites of eggs with three tablespoonfuls of sugar to a stiff froth, put on top of custard and bake a delicate brown.

Mrs. Gage Carlin.

COCOANUT PIE.

One grated cocoanut, one quart of milk, three eggs, one tablespoonful of butter, one cupful of sugar; beat yolks and sugar, add three tablespoonfuls of flour. Cook cocoanut, milk, sugar, and yolks together, then add the beaten whites of the eggs. This will make two large pies.

Mrs. H. S. Taylor.

LEMON PIE.

Juice and grated rind of two lemons, two cupfuls of boiling water, two cupfuls of sugar, one scant teacupful of butter, two eggs, two tablespoonfuls of corn starch. Wet corn starch with cold water and stir into the boiling water. when it boils, pour over the sugar lemon and butter; when cool add the eggs. Bake with two crusts, or with a meringue on top.

Mrs. A. Letson.

CHOCOLATE PIE.

Three-fourths of a pint of milk, four tablespoonfuls of sugar, one heaping tablespoonful of flour, rubbed smooth, yolks of two eggs beaten with flour, three tablespoonfuls of chocolate, one tablespoonful of sugar. Put chocolate, sugar and a little water on stove to dissolve. Put milk and sugar on stove and let get hot, then add eggs and flour, stirring until thick. Stir in chocolate and one teaspoonful of vanilla. Pour into pie crust which has been baked and cover custard with meringue made from whites of eggs with three tablespoonfuls of sugar.

Mrs. Gafe

PEACH PIE.

Peel, stone, and slice the peaches; line a pie plate with a rich crust, lay in the fruit, sprinkling each layer with sugar in proportion to their sweetness, and small pieces of butter. If peaches are not very juicy, add a *little* water. Bake with an upper crust.

Miss Hoge.

CHERRY PIE.

Line the pie-pan with with a rich crust, fill with ripe cherries which have been stoned; sprinkle well with sugar, regulating the quantity of sugar by their sweetness. Cover with an upper crust, and bake. Sift white sugar over the top. Eat cold.

Blackberry, raspberry, and plum pies are made in the same manner.

Miss Hoge.

CUSTARD PIE.

Line your pie-pans with crust. Beat four eggs with a tablespoonful of sugar to each egg, pour over them one quart of scalding milk, stir and pour into the pans, grate nutmeg over the top and bake fifteen minutes.

Mrs. W. Powell.

~~~~~~~~~~

SAUCES FOR PUDDINGS.

HARD SAUCE.

One cupful of sugar, half a cupful of butter, a little grated nutmeg, two tablespoonfuls of wine, brandy, or lemon juice.

<div align="right">Mrs. W. S. Robinson</div>

RAISIN SAUCE.

One cupful of raisins, one-half pint of water and one-half cupful of sugar. Stir one-half hour or until tender. There should be a cupful of the syrup when cooked; add butter size of a walnut and two teaspoonfuls of flour rubbed smooth. This is nice for rice and bread puddings.

<div align="right">Mrs. Gage</div>

CUSTARD.

One pint of milk, three eggs, one cupful of sugar, pinch of salt. Bring milk to a boil; beat eggs and sugar together, stir into the boiling milk, add the salt, flavor with vanilla. Boil until thick as cream.

PLUM PUDDING SAUCE.

One teacupful of butter with one pint of powdered sugar, and one teaspoonful of flour rubbed to a cream. Pour on just before serving one-half pint of boiling water, and add flavoring.

Mrs. Gage.

HARD PLUM PUDDING SAUCE.

One teacupful of butter with one pint of pulverized sugar rubbed to a cream, add the whites of two eggs beaten to a stiff froth, then one-half cupful of brandy.

Mrs. Gage.

LEMON SAUCE.

One cupful of sugar, one-half cupful of water, the rind and juice of two lemons, yolks of three eggs. Boil together the sugar, lemon, and water, for twenty minutes. Beat the yolks of eggs; put the basin containing the syrup into another of boiling water. Stir the yolks into this and beat rapidly three minutes. Take off the fire and continue beating for five minutes.

Miss Hoge.

WINE SAUCE.

One cupful of butter, two cupfuls of powdered sugar, one half cupful of wine. Beat butter to a cream, add sugar gradually, and when very light, add the wine, which has been made hot, a little at a time. Place the bowl in a basin of hot water and stir for two minutes.

Miss Hoge.

CLEAR SAUCE.

Half a cupful of butter, one tablespoonful of flour, two and a half cupfuls of sugar. Rub flour and sugar together, then add the butter, pour a cupful of boiling water over it, and boil until waxy, add then half a cupful of wine.

Miss Hoge.

CABINET SAUCE.

Yolks of three eggs whipped very light, one lemon, juice and half the grated rind, one glass of wine, one teaspoonful of cinnamon, one cup of sugar, one tablespoonful of butter. Rub the butter and sugar together, add yolks, lemon and spice; beat well, put in the wine, still stirring hard. Set in a sauce-pan of boiling water, and beat while it heats, but do not let it boil.

Miss Hoge.

LEMON SAUCE No. 2.

One cup of sugar, butter the size of an egg, one egg, one lemon, —all the juice and half the grated rind, one teaspoonful of nutmeg three tablespoonfuls of boiling water. Cream the butter and sugar, beat in the egg whipped light; lemon and nutmeg. Beat hard ten minutes, add the boiling water a spoonful at a time. Heat *very* hot, but do not boil. Stir constantly.

Miss Hoge

FOAMY SAUCE.

Rub one-half cupful of butter to a cream, adding slowly one cupful of sugar, one teaspoonful of vanilla, two teaspoonfuls of wine or fruit juice. Just before serving add one-fourth cupful of boiling water. Stir well, then add white of one egg beaten to a froth and serve at once.

Miss Dodge.

DESSERTS.

SAGO PUDDING.

Take one cupful of sago and soak a few minutes, one cupful of raisins stewed a very little, have a vessel with one quart of boiling water, add a little salt and stir in the sago, and then the raisins with the water in which they were stewed, one cupful of sugar and a little nutmeg, dissolve a little jelly in the water before the sago is added; cook five minutes, stirring constantly.

Miss Lewis.

TAPIOCA PUDDING.

To one cupful of tapioca take one quart of water and soak over night, the next day add two and one-half cupfuls of brown sugar bake in an oven until it thickens like taffy—say thirty minutes. when nearly cold add one tablespoonful of vanilla. Fresh pineapple cut in shape of dice and added when vanilla is added makes a nice change; serve with cream.

Mrs. Milton Taylor.

FRUIT TAPIOCA.

Soak a cupful of tapioca over night; in the morning pour on a pint and a half of boiling water, two-thirds of a cupful of sugar, boil an hour or until like jelly. stir in just before taking off the fire, raspberry or strawberry jam or fresh fruit.

Mrs. Innes.

BAKED APPLE AND TAPIOCA.

One-half cupful of tapioca soaked over night. pour on a pint of boiling water and two thirds cup of sugar, boil until the consistency of jelly; have half a dozen apples roasting in the oven, about fifteen minutes before they are done pour over them the tapioca and bake for fifteen minutes. Flavor the tapioca with *zest*.

Mrs. Benner.

APPLE TAPIOCA.

One large coffee cup tapioca soaked over night, one-quarter peck of apples pared and cut in small slices, then put in porcelain kettle and stewed until smooth, drain tapioca and stir in slowly, cooking until clear, stirring all the time, sugar to taste; with good cooking apples ten minutes will be sufficient, flavor with nutmeg or not, as desired; pour into molds which have been dipped in cold water.

Miss Matthews.

CHARLOTTE RUSSE.

One pint of cream whipped, one-half box of gelatine dissolved in one pint of sweet milk; before beating cream sweeten with one-half cupful of sugar, whites of two eggs beaten to a froth with a little sugar, add eggs, milk and gelatine to cream, beating all the time, and flavor with vanilla, sherry wine or almond extract; if almond is used be careful not to use but a little, pour in mould and put on ice, serve with whipped cream.

Mrs. Gage.

BABA.

Sponge cake baked in turk's head pan—any recipe will do, must be dry, at least three days old; turn upside down, make incisions with knife, pouring into incisions rum or brandy, three tablespoonfuls to a cake; ice with any sort of icing, but ice thoroughly, remembering that bottom of sponge cake is to be the top of *Baba;* on this icing put in regular rows almonds blanched and split. *Baba* is prettier if put on flat dish considerably larger than cake; fill tunnel shaped opening of cake with whipped cream, whipped very stiff, heap cream also around base of cake, over *all* the cream scatter candied fruits, cherries and citron in forms of pears and strawberries, etc. Materials needed for one large or two small cakes are: One pint of cream one-half pound of candied fruits, one pound of almonds, four ounces of rum or sherry and as much again if desired mingled with whipped cream. One small cake is enough for ten people.

Miss Warder.

CHARLOTTE RUSSE.

Two cups flour, two cups sugar, four eggs, two-thirds cup boiling water (added to sugar and yolks), one teaspoonful cream of tartar, one-half teaspoonful soda, add whites beaten stiff last; spread thinly on biscuit tins, cut in strips and fit in oval tin or paper moulds. Filling—one scant ounce of Cox's gelatine soaked in one tea cup of cold water for an hour or more, set vessel in hot water to dissolve; make a custard of one and a half cups of milk, four yolks, one tea cup of sugar, when cool add the dissolved gelatine, then one tea cup of wine, one tea cup of sugar, then whites of four eggs beaten stiff, last one pint of rich cream, flavor with vanilla. Congeals best on ice.

Miss Matthews.

SPANISH CREAM.

One quart of milk, yellows of three eggs, one-half cupful of sugar, one-half box of gelatine, put milk and gelatine together on top of stove and let get scalding hot, beat eggs and sugar together until light and add to milk, leave on stove five minutes, turn into a mould after adding one teaspoonful of vanilla. Serve with whipped cream.
Miss Robinson.

APPLE SNOW.

Pare, core and bring to a boil in as little water as possible six tart apples, cool, strain, beat well and add the whipped whites of three eggs, sweeten to taste, beat fifteen minutes, flavor with lemon juice and serve with whipped cream.
Mrs. Hoge.

ORANGE CREAM.

Juice of six oranges, quarter pound of sugar, one pint of boiling water and six eggs; beat the yolks, add sugar, orange juice and water, stir over the fire until it thickens, pour in a mould and when cool put on the top the beaten whites of two eggs, sweetened and flavored with a little of the rind.
Miss Hoge.

AMERICAN MERINGUE.

One quart of milk, yolks of three eggs, one-half cupful of sugar, one-half box of gelatine; put milk and gelatine on the stove and let get scalding hot, beat eggs and sugar until light and add to milk; leave on stove five minutes and flavor with one-half cupful of sugar put in a small frying pan and stirred over the fire until the sugar turns liquid and begins to smoke; then add to hot mixture, turn into a mould and (when cold) serve with red raspberry jam and whipped cream.

Miss Robinson.

LEMON SPONGE.

The juice of four lemons, four eggs, one cupful of sugar, one-third box of gelatine, one pint cold water; soak the gelatine two hours in half a cupful of the water, squeeze the lemons and strain the juice on the sugar, beat the yolks of the eggs and mix them with the remainder of the water; add the sugar and lemon to this and cook in the double boiler until it begins to thicken, then add the gelatine; strain this into a tin basin, which place in a pan of ice water, beat with a whisk occasionally until it has cooled but not hardened; now add the unbeaten whites of the eggs, and beat all the time until the mixture begins to thicken; remember that the whites of the eggs must be added as soon as the mixture cools, which should be in about eight minutes; pour at once into moulds which have previously been wet with cold water, serve with cream and sugar.

WHITE JELLY.

Put on to boil in a water bath one pint of sweet milk, new is the best. When scalding hot add to it one ounce of Cox's gelatine which has soaked one hour in a coffee cupful of water. Stir until dissolved, then add one tablespoonful of sugar and flavor with vanilla, sherry, or sherry and rum mixed. Turn into a mould.

Miss. E. Warder.

PEACH CUSTARD.

Pare, and cut in quarters one dozen fine, ripe peaches, sprinkle with four tablespoonfuls of sugar. Let them stand about five minutes on ice. Put the peaches in a glass dish, and pour over a rich custard. Set on ice until ready to serve.

Miss Hoge.

ORANGE SPONGE.

Make orange sponge the same as lemon, using a small pint of water and the juice of six large oranges.

FROZEN WHIPPED CREAM.

Sweeten the cream and flavor with *zest*; whip *very stiff*, then freeze.

Mrs H. S. Taylor.

SARATOGA ITALIAN CREAM.

One ounce of gelatine soaked in a little water two hours, then melted; strain and let stand until nearly cold. One pint of the best cream put in a deep dish with the juice of two lemons, two oranges and part of the grated rind, two glasses of sherry wine, three-fourths pound of powdered sugar. The cream must be well whipped, then slowly add wine, sugar and gelatine. Turn in mould and when cold serve with whipped cream.

Miss Philips.

ORANGE JELLY.

Two-thirds of an ounce of gelatine covered with one-half pint of cold water, and let dissolve. Add three cupfuls of sugar, the juice of four lemons and the juice of four or six oranges. Peel and slice the four oranges and line glass dish. Then strain jelly, after adding one pint of boiling water, over the sliced oranges. To make wine jelly add one-half pint of wine to recipe, omitting the sliced oranges.

Mrs. Merrill Miller.

WINE JELLY.

Three cupfuls of sugar, one of cold water, one pint of sherry, one package of gelatine, juice of two lemons, one quart of boiling water, add wine, lemon juice, and sugar. Pour into a mould that has previously been wet with cold water. Malaga grapes and sliced oranges mixed through the jelly, add to the taste and looks.

MISS HOGE.

RUSSIA CREAM.

One quart of milk, four eggs, one-half box of gelatine, one teacupful of sugar. Pour half the milk over the gelatine, set in the oven to dissolve. When dissolved add sugar, put in a sauce-pan of hot water, and let it come to a boil. Beat the yolks and add to the other pint of milk, add to the boiling milk. Set away to cool. Stir in the beaten whites when almost cool, flavor, and pour in moulds.

MISS HEDGES.

ORANGE SOUFFLÉ.

Four oranges cut in pieces, two-thirds of a cupful of white sugar sprinkled over them, yolks of three eggs, one tablespoonful of corn starch, one pint of sweet milk made into a custard, and when cool pour over the oranges. The whites of the eggs beaten with one cup of sugar, spread over all and brown in the oven.

MRS. LEIGHTON.

PINEAPPLE CREAM.

One pint of canned pineapple, one teacup of sugar, one pint of cream, one-half box of gelatine, one-half cup of cold water. Dissolve the gelatine in the water. Chop the pineapple fine, put it on the stove with the sugar; simmer twenty minutes; add the gelatine and strain. Beat until it begins to thicken, add the cream which has been whipped to a froth. When all mixed pour into a mould to harden.

MISS THOMSON.

BANANA FLOAT.

Take one box of Cox's gelatine and dissolve in one cup of cold water. Three pints of rich sweet milk, two and a half cups of of sugar. Boil and when boiled dip out as much as will finish dissolving the gelatine. When all is dissolved, pour in the rest of the milk and boil ten minutes. When cold but not stiff, stir in six bananas, which have been previously cut up with a silver fork. Mix well and set on ice, or in a cool place. An hour before serving, take a quart of rich cream, whip stiff, flavor and sweeten to taste, and pour around the above mixture.

MISS JULIA AYERS.

FLOAT.

One quart of milk, one pint of cream, ten eggs, four tablespoonfuls of sugar, teaspoonful of flavoring, whites of eggs beaten to a stiff froth; slightly cooked in scalding milk, and kept in cool place till time for using. Custard of the well beaten yolks, sugar, cream and milk allowed to come to a boil, flavor when cold.

MRS. THOMSON.

FIG PUDDING.

One-half pound of figs, one-half pound of bread crumbs, six ounces of moist sugar (wet the sugar before weighing), six ounces beef suet, two eggs, a little nutmeg, a cup of milk, figs and sugar to be chopped very fine, mix all together and steam in mould or steamer two hours; serve with sauce.

MRS. T. J. CANTWELL.

FROZEN APRICOTS.

One can of apricots, three-fourths of a pint of sugar, a quart of water, a pint of cream after it is whipped; cut the apricots in small pieces, add the sugar and water, and freeze, when partially frozen add the cream; use only the peeled apricots.

MRS. INNES.

SNOW PUDDING.

Dissolve one-fourth box of gelatine in one-half cupful of cold water about an hour, then fill up the cup with boiling water to dissolve thoroughly, put the whites of three eggs into a big bowl but do not beat, add to them the juice of one lemon, two scant cupfuls of sugar and the gelatine; beat half an hour; if it grows too stiff add a little water, put in mould and serve with sauce made as follows: Two cupfuls of milk, yolks of three eggs, three tablespoonfuls of sugar, flavoring; scald the milk, add sugar and eggs, and boil until like float; sauce and pudding to be rather cold.

Mrs T. J. Cantwell.

SNOW PUDDING.

One-third box of gelatine dissolved in a little cold water, and when softened stir into it one pint of boiling water, one cupful of sugar and the juice of three lemons (if not very juicy add more). When cold and beginning to thicken add the well beaten whites of three eggs, beat all lightly and smoothly together and pour into a mould to harden; serve with boiled custard.

Miss Robinson

FROZEN PEACHES.

One can of peaches, three-fourths pint of sugar, two cupfuls of cream—after it is whipped; boil sugar and water together for ten minutes, add peaches and cook twenty minutes longer, cut the peaches in small pieces before cooking them, when they are partially frozen add whipped cream.

Mrs. Innes.

CLARET PUNCH.

The juice of six lemons, one quart of water, sweeten to taste, one tablespoonful of gelatine, soak gelatine in a little of the water, boil one cupful of the water and dissolve the gelatine in it, mix together the sugar, water, gelatine, lemon juice and one pint of claret, then freeze.

Mrs. Innes.

CARAMEL ICE CREAM.

One pound of brown sugar melted and slightly scorched, stir and add one pint of boiling cream, beat the whites of three eggs, add three tablespoonfuls of powdered sugar, stir in the boiling milk and sugar; add one tablespoonful of vanilla, set away to cool, then freeze.

Miss Kate Fisher.

RASPBERRY SHERBET AND CHARLOTTE RUSSE.

Sherbet—one pint of preserved fruit, one cup of sugar, one quart of water, two lemons, one tablespoonful of gelatine, soak fruit in part of the water and strain out the seeds, soak gelatine in one-fourth cupful of cold water, then add half cupful of boiling water to finish dissolving, mix all together and freeze; have your charlotte russe made, put alternate layers of sherbet and charlotte russe in a tin box, pack in ice an hour before using.

Mrs. Swartz.

COFFEE JELLY.

One pint of coffee, three-fourths pint of sugar, half pint of cold water a box of gelatine, juice of one lemon, soak gelatine two hours in the cold water, pour the boiling water upon it; when dissolved add sugar, coffee and lemon juice, turn into mould and set away to cool, eat with cream and sugar; sufficient for twelve persons.

Mrs. Innes.

LEMON ICE.

Boil three pints of water and one pound of sugar until reduced to about one quart, when cold add the juice of eight lemons and the thin sliced yellow part, let stand half an hour, strain without pressing; when nearly frozen stir in lightly the beaten whites of two eggs.

Miss Hoge.

ORANGE ICE.

Juice of seven oranges, grated peel of three, juice of five lemons, three pounds of sugar, one gallon of water, whites of two eggs beaten in when half frozen. Serve in orange skins.

Miss Hoge.

AMBROSIA.

Seven sweet oranges peeled and sliced, one half of a grated cocoanut, put in layers, and sprinkle with powdered sugar.

Miss Hoge.

CURRANT ICE.

Boil one quart of water and one pound of sugar until reduced to about one pint, add one pint of currant juice; when partly frozen add the beaten whites of two eggs. A good ice for fever patients.

Miss Hoge.

TUTTI FRUTTI.

Make either Mrs. Robinson's or the above recipe for ice cream and flavor with two tablespoonfuls of Sicily Madeira wine or Maraschina; when partly frozen add one pound of French candied fruit, cut fine; use a mixture of cherries, plums, apricots, pineapples pears, strawberries and angelica root, or use home-made preserves carefully drained from syrup and cut into dice.

Miss Sarah MacConnell.

BANANA ICE CREAM.

Make a custard with one pint of milk, two cups of sugar, and two eggs; when cold add one pint of cream and six bananas mashed or cut into thin slices. Add lemon juice if the bananas lack flavor. Freeze.

Miss Philips.

FROZEN PUDDING.

One generous pint of milk, two cupfuls of granulated sugar, two eggs, three tablespoonfuls of gelatine, one quart of cream, eight tablespoonfuls of sherry wine, one pound of candied cherries; let the milk come to a boil; beat one cupful of sugar and eggs together and stir into the boiling milk, boil twenty minutes, then add the gelatine which has been soaking one or two hours in just enough water to cover it, set away to cool, when cool add the other cup of sugar, wine and cream; when set in the freezer add fruit, can be used without fruit.   Mrs. Innes.

PINEAPPLE SHERBET.

Soak two tablespoonfuls of gelatine in two cupfuls of cold water, finish dissolving in two cupfuls of boiling water, add one pint of sugar, juice of four lemons, and one can of grated pineapple; serve in orange or lemon skins.

Miss Hoge.

ICE CREAM.

One gallon of cream, two and a half cups of sugar, two tablespoonfuls of gelatine soaked two hours in milk (and then melted in a double boiler), one tablespoonful of vanilla; after it commences to freeze beat with a spoon.   Mrs. J. S. Robinson.

NESSELRODE PUDDING.

Shell one pint of chestnuts, blanch, boil one-half an hour, mash to a pulp and stir into ice cream strain, and when partly frozen add one pint of mixed fruit, cut fine.

Miss Phillips (Miss Sarah MacConnell.)

PINEAPPLE ICE CREAM.

Two quarts of cream, one pineapple grated, two and a half cups of sugar, one tablespoonful of gelatine dissolved in milk. When cream is partly frozen add fruit.

Miss Gage.

TUTTI FRUTTI ICE CREAM.

One generous pint of rich milk, two cupfuls of granulated sugar, two eggs, three tablespoonfuls of gelatine, one quart of cream, two teaspoonfuls of vanilla; when the cream is partly frozen add cherries, currants, citron, and any other candied fruit that you wish. Add the same quantity of fruit as there is of ice cream. Let the milk come to a boil; beat one cupful of the sugar and the eggs together, and stir into the boiling milk; cook twenty minutes; then add the gelatine which has been cooking an hour or two in just enough water to cover it. Remove from the fire. When cool add the other cupful of sugar and the cream which has been whipped. Freeze.

Miss Hoge.

CARAMEL ICE-CREAM.

One generous pint of milk, two cupfuls of granulated sugar, two tablespoonfuls of flour, two tablespoonfuls of gelatine, one quart of cream. Let the milk come to a boil; beat the two eggs, one cupful of sugar and flour together and add to boiling milk. Cook ten minutes in double boiler, and add the gelatine, which has been soaking two hours in a little water; flavor with the caramel while the custard is hot. To make the caramel take one cupful of sugar and put in fryingpan and stir over the fire until the sugar turns liquid and begins to smoke, then turn in custard. Let to cool, add one quart of whipped cream and freeze. The flavor of this cream can be varried by browning the sugar more or less.

Miss Robinson.

STRAWBERRY ICE CREAM.

Two quarts of cream, two quarts of fresh berries put through the colander, three cupfuls of sugar, one generous tablespoonful of gelatine dissolved in a little milk. Add sweetened berries to cream when partly frozen.

Miss Robinson.

CHOCOLATE ICE CREAM.

Make custard as for frozen pudding, and add to the boiling mixture two squares of chocolate (scrape the squares of chocolate and add four tablespoonfuls of sugar and two of boiling water. Stir this over the fire until smooth.) Let cool add whipped cream and freeze.

BANANA ICE CREAM.

Two quarts of cream, two cupfuls of sugar, eight bananas, one large tablespoonful of gelatine, dissolved in a little milk and allowed to cool. Mash bananas with a silver spoon and add to sugar, cream, and gelatine. Put a little of the sugar with bananas.

Miss Robinson.

PEACH ICE CREAM.

Two quarts of cream, two and a half cupfuls of sugar, one quart of sliced peaches (canned peaches can be used but are not as nice) one tablespoonful of gelatine dissolved in milk. Press the peaches with a little of the sugar through the colander; add to the cream after it is partly frozen. Apricots, raspberries, oranges, or any fruit you wish can be used.

Miss Philips.

ALMOND CUSTARD.

One pint of rich milk, one-fourth pound of blanched almonds (pounded to a paste), one teaspoonful of vanilla, yolks of three eggs, four tablespoonfuls of sugar, one teaspoonful of extract of bitter almonds in the meringue. Scald the milk, add the beaten yolks, the sugar, almond paste. Boil, stirring constantly until it thickens. Stir up well; when almost cold pour into cups. Make a meringue of the whites of two eggs and two tablespoonfuls of powdered sugar, flavored with bitter almond. Heap upon each cup.

Miss Geraldine Hoge.

FLOATING ISLAND.

One quart of new milk, yolks of five eggs, five tablespoonfuls of sugar, two teaspoonfuls of vanilla or bitter almond extract. Beat the yolks well, stir in the sugar, and add the hot, *not* boiling milk, a little at a time. Boil until it begins to thicken. When cool, flavor and pour into a glass dish. Before serving add a teacupful of whipped cream. You can make a meringue of the whites of two of the eggs and two tablespoonfuls of powdered sugar.

Miss Hoge.

ROMAN PUNCH.

One pound of loaf sugar, one large cupful of strong black tea (made), two wine glasses of brandy and one of rum, one bottle of of champagne, juice of three oranges, juice of three lemons. Mix well together, and freeze.

Mrs. Hoge.

BLANCE-MANGE WITH GELATINE.

One-third package of gelatine, one quart of milk, one teacupful of sugar, pinch of salt, one-fourth teaspoonful of almond extract. Put the gelatine with a little of the milk and let stand two hours, then put milk with gelatine in double boiler and let get scalding hot; as soon as the gelatine is melted take from fire, add sugar, salt and flavoring. Strain and turn into mould. Serve with cream.

JUDGE PETER'S PUDDING.

Three-fourths box of gelatine, two oranges, two bananas, six figs, two lemons, ten English walnuts. Dissolve the gelatine in one-half pint of cold water, then add one-half pint of boiling water, the juice of two lemons, two cupfuls of powdered sugar; strain and let stand until it begins to thicken. Stir in the fruit, cut in small pieces and turn into a mould and let harden. Serve with whipped cream. More lemon juice will be an improvement for many.

Miss Stone.

BLANC-MANGE.

One quart of new milk, three tablespoonfuls of corn starch, one teacupful of sugar, pinch of salt; wet corn starch with a little milk. Add to the boiling milk the sugar, salt and corn starch, boil five minutes and when taken from stove, add flavoring and turn into mould. Serve with cream.

Miss Hoge.

PRUNE PUDDING.

One-fourth of a pound of raisins stoned; stew in water enough to cover them. Beat whites of five eggs to a stiff froth with one-half cupful of powdered sugar, add one-fourth teaspoonful of cream tartar; put into an earthen pudding dish and bake twenty-two minutes in a slow oven. Serve with soft custard.

Miss Mary Powell.

CAKES.

CAKE.

Use the best materials for making cake. Always beat eggs separately and add the whites the last thing. Mix baking powder in flour. First cream the butter and sugar, then add alternately flour and milk. Have a steady heat. To test whether a cake is done, run a straw into the thickest part; it should come up clean.

Miss Hoge.

GINGER SPONGE CAKE.

One cup of molasses, one cup of butter, two cups of sugar, three cups of flour, four eggs, two tablespoonfuls of ginger, one cup of sour milk with one teaspoonful of soda dissolved in it. Add juice and rind of one large or two small lemons.

Miss Matthews.

WHITE FRUIT CAKE.

Three cups of sugar, two cups of butter, one cup of sweet milk, five cups of flour, two teaspoonfuls of Royal Baking Powder, two teaspoonfuls of lemon extract, three-fourths of a pound of seeded raisins, three-fourth of a pound of citron, one-fourth of a pound of blanched almonds, one-fourth of a pound of grated cocoanut, one wine glassful of brandy, whites of eight eggs. Add fruit and brandy after the flour. Bake slowly.

Miss Hoge.

ICE-CREAM CAKE.

Two cupfuls of sugar, on cupful of butter, one cupful of milk, one cupful of corn starch, two cupfuls of flour, two teaspoonfuls of Royal Baking Powder, whites of eight eggs.

Mrs. Swartz.

WHITE ICING.

On two cupfuls of sugar, pour one-half pint of boiling water; boil (do not stir) until clear and waxy. Pour this on the beaten whites of two eggs. Flavor with lemon juice. Beat until cool.

Miss Hoge.

CHOCOLATE ICING.

Two cupfuls of white sugar, one cupful of milk, one cupful of grated chocolate, butter size of a hickory nut; boil fifteen minutes, add one teaspoonful of vanilla.

Miss Robinson.

SNOW CAKE.

Whites of ten eggs, one and one-half tumblerfuls of granulated sugar, one tumblerful of flour, one teaspoonful of cream-tartar stirred into the flour. Beat the whites to a stiff froth, add the sugar, then the flour. Beat just enough to mix well. Flavor with lemon.

Mrs. Phillips.

VANITY CAKE.

One and one-half cupfuls of sugar, one-half cupful of butter, one-half cupful of milk, one and one-half cupfuls of flour, one-half cupful of corn starch, one teaspoonful Royal Baking Powder; bake in two layers, use any kind of icing. Mrs. Damon.

NUT CAKE.

Two cupfuls of sugar, one cupful of butter, three cupfuls of flour, one cupful of cold water, four eggs, two cupfuls of nuts (hickory), three teaspoonfuls of Royal baking powder.

Mrs. Childs.

SPONGE CAKE.

Two cupfuls of sugar, one cupful of flour, one-half cupful of water two teaspoonfuls of Royal baking powder, six eggs. Beat yolks and sugar together, add water, flour and lastly the beaten whites.

Mrs. Damon.

CHOCOLATE CAKE.

Two cupfuls of brown sugar, one cupful of butter, two cupfuls of flour, one and one-half cupfuls of grated chocolate, one-half cupful of sweet milk with one teaspoonful of *soda* dissolved in it, whites and yolks of four eggs. Bake in jelly cake pans, ice with white icing.

Miss V. Hoge.

COFFEE CAKE.

One cupful of butter, two of sugar (dark brown), one of Orleans molasses, one of coffee, four and a half of flour, which allows for that on fruit, three eggs, one cupful of currants, one of seeded raisins, one-half of citron, one-half of whisky, two tablespoonfuls of cloves, three of cinnamon, one teaspoonful of soda, or three of Royal Baking Powder; mix as fruit cake is mixed, and bake.

Mrs. Robinson.

GINGER DROP-CAKES.

One cupful of molasses, or maple syrup, one-half cupful of sour milk with one half teaspoonful of soda dissolved in it, ginger and other spices, flour enough to thicken. Drop in a greased pan and bake quickly.

Miss Hoge.

ORANGE SPONGE CAKE.

One coffee cupful of sugar, one coffee cupful of flour, four eggs beaten separately, one teaspoonful of Royar baking powder, pinch of salt, juice of one small orange, and half the grated rind.

Mrs. Hoge.

JUMBLES.

One coffee cupful of sugar, three-fourths of a cupful of butter, one-fourth cupful of sour milk, one scant teaspoonful of soda, two eggs, half a teaspoonful of salt, nutmeg to taste, enough flour to make a soft dough. Roll and cut out with a cake cutter.

Mrs. Hoge.

ALMOND TART.

One pound of shelled almonds grated, sixteen eggs, one pound of pulverized sugar; beat sugar and yellows of eggs together until light, add juice of one-half lemon with grated rind, two tablespoonfuls of sifted corn starch with the almond flour, beat all three-fourths of an hour, bake on pan that opens, and leave on bottom, as it spoils it to turn it out.

Mrs. Robinson.

GINGER POUND CAKE.

One cup of brown sugar, one cup of molasses, one cup of butter, one teaspoonful of soda dissolved in two tablespoonfuls of sour milk or hot water, five eggs, one teaspoonful of salt, one of cloves, one of cinnamon, one tablespoonful of ginger, three cups of flour.

Miss Hoge.

SOUR CREAM CAKE.

One cupful of butter, two of sugar, one of milk, two teaspoonfuls of Royal Baking Powder, three cupfuls of flour, whites of six eggs, one teaspoonful of vanilla; bake in jelly-cake pans.

Cream for filling.—One pint of rich sour cream, beaten until it becomes thick, three eggs, beaten separately, one-half cupful of sugar, one pound of almonds, blanched and beaten fine, three teaspoonfuls of vanilla, add the eggs last, spread between the layers of cake.

Mrs. Bomford, U. S. A.

CREAM CAKE.

Six eggs, two cupfuls of sugar, two heaping teaspoonfuls of Royal Baking Powder, two cupfuls of unsifted flour, one-fourth cupful of sweet milk, a little nutmeg, beat yolks of eggs and sugar until light, add other ingredients and beat twenty minutes. This will make three layers.

Mrs. Gage.

CREAM FOR LAYER CAKE.

One quart of milk, butter size of an egg, one and a half heaping tablespoonfuls of flour, one-half cupful of sugar, wet flour with milk and rub until smooth, put in double boiler and boil one minute, spread between layers and on top; over top layer sift a little powdered sugar.

NUT CAKE.

One cupful of butter worked to a cream, two and one-half of sugar mixed with butter, one cupful of sweet milk, three and one-half of flour, and one-half of brandy, four eggs, yolks with butter and sugar, three teaspoonfuls of Royal Baking Powder, one pint of hickory or almond kernels, one pound of seeded raisins.

Miss Robinson.

CREAM FOR LAYER CAKE.

Beat one-half cup of sugar and one egg together, add three tablespoonfuls of flour, when thoroughly beaten pour in one cupful of boiling milk, keep stirring until thick; flavor to taste.

Miss Hoge.

WHITE CAKE.

Three cupfuls of sugar, one *full* cup of butter, one and a half cupfuls of sweet milk, whites of twelve eggs, beaten to a froth, four and a half cupfuls of flour, and one-half cupful of corn starch, three teaspoonfuls of Royal Baking Powder; flavor with vanilla or lemon, cream, butter and sugar, add a little milk, then flour, until all the milk is used, then add one-half of the beaten whites, the rest of the flour and the other half of the eggs; bake in moderate oven from one and a quarter to one and a half hours.

Mrs. Robinson.

RAISED DOUGHNUTS.

Two cupfuls of sugar, one of butter, two of milk, one of yeast, three eggs, and a little nutmeg; make a batter and let rise until morning, make into dough and let rise again, cut into shape, let rise until light, and then fry; while still hot roll in powdered sugar.

Mrs. Robinson.

LOAF CAKE.

Three cupfuls of bread dough, one cupful of butter, three scant cupfuls of sugar, one cupful of raisins seeded, one cupful of English currants, three eggs, one teaspoonful of soda, one-half nutmeg, grated, two teaspoonfuls of cinnamon, one-half teaspoonful of cloves, and one wine glassful of brandy or whisky; mix butter and sugar to a cream, add eggs well beaten and then dough, stir well, then add spices and brandy, and if the dough is very soft add an extra cupful of flour; grease the pan and pour in the mixture let it rise four hours, bake from one and a half to two hours.

Mrs. Robinson.

EASY CAKE.

One cupful of sugar, one-half cupful of butter, one-half cupful of sweet milk, three eggs, two cupfuls of flour, one spoonful of Royal baking powder. Eat while fresh,

Miss Hoge.

MOUNTAIN CAKE.

Two cupfuls of sugar, two thirds cupful butter, three and one-half cupfuls flour, one cupful of milk, three teaspoonfuls of Royal Baking Powder, whites of six eggs, mix as soft as possible; will make three layers.   Miss Lillie McConnell.

MARBLE CAKE.

Dark Part—One cupful of butter, two cupfuls of brown sugar, one cupful of molasses, one cupful of strong coffee, yolks of eight eggs, four and a half cupfuls of flour, two teaspoonfuls of soda sifted in the flour, two teaspoonfuls of cloves, two teaspoonfuls of cinnamon, one teaspoonful of mace, one pound of raisins, seeded, one pound of English currants; three-fourths pound of citron.

White part—One cup of butter, four cups of sugar, two cups of sweet milk, four cups of flour, two cups of corn starch, whites of eight eggs beaten to a froth, four teaspoonfuls of Royal Baking Powder sifted with the flour, flavor with vanilla, use teacup for measuring; put one spoonful of light dough in pan and then one spoonful of dark until the pan is almost filled. This recipe will make two cakes. It will keep for weeks.

Miss Lillie McConnell.

SPRINGFIELD ALMOND CAKE.

Two cupfuls of sugar, one of butter and one of milk, four of flour, five eggs, two teaspoonfuls cream of tartar, and one of soda; bake in jelly cake pans. Make a custard, one cup of sour cream, one egg, one-half pound of almonds, blanched and chopped fine, one tablespoonful of sugar; flavor with sherry. Do not spread until cake is cold.

Miss Sarah MacConnell.

HICKORY NUT MACAROONS.

One quart of hickory nut kernels, picked out, one pound of granulated sugar, whites of three eggs, half a cup of flour; make cold icing with eggs and sugar, roll nuts with rolling pin, sift flour over them, make into balls the size of a hickory nut, or drop with spoon, onto buttered paper, put on top of a narrow pan and bake in a very *cool* oven, as for kisses.

Miss Philips.

SOFT COOKIES.

Two cups of sugar, one cup of butter, three eggs, one-half cup of sour milk; one-half teaspoonful of soda dissolved in the milk, two tablespoonfuls of cinnamon, five cups of flour. Roll as soft as possible. Bake in a quick oven.

Miss Philips.

CHOCOLATE COOKIES.

One cup of butter, two cups of sugar, three cups of flour, four eggs, one cup of grated chocolate, one-half teaspoonful of soda. Roll thin. Better with age.

Miss Leighton.

CHOCOLATE ICING.

Two squares of Baker's chocolate, the whites of two eggs, two cupfuls powdered sugar, four tablespoonfuls boiling water; beat one and two-thirds cupfuls of the sugar into the unbeaten whites of the eggs, scrape the chocolate and put it and the remaining one-third cupful of sugar and the water in a pan; stir over a hot fire until smooth and glossy, then stir into the beaten whites and sugar.

Miss Powell.

CRULLERS.

Two cups sugar, one cup sour milk, one teaspoonful soda, three eggs, lump of butter the size of an egg, flour enough to make a stiff dough; cut out and fry in boiling lard. Sift powdered sugar over them while hot.

Mrs. J. S. Robinson

MAPLE FROSTING.

One cupful maple syrup, boiled until waxy; beat the the white of one egg to a stiff froth, pour on the syrup, and beat until cool.

Mrs. Swartz.

FRENCH CAKE.

Two cups sugar, one-half cup butter, three cups flour, two teaspoonfuls Royal Baking Powder, one cup of cold water. Flavor with lemon.

Miss Minnie Damon.

ENGLISH BUNN CAKE.

One pint sugar, one pint flour, one cupful butter, one cupful sweet milk, one tablespoonful cinnamon, and one-half teaspoonful of cloves, two teaspoonfuls Royal Baking Powder, four eggs leaving out the whites of two for icing.

Miss Leigh.

SAND TARTS.

One pound sugar, one pound flour, one-half pound butter, five tablespoonfuls sweet milk, one heaping teaspoonful Royal Baking Powder, yolks of seven eggs; roll out a little thicker than pie crust, cut in squares about three inches, spread with the white of egg, sprinkle with sugar and cinnamon and stick with one or more almonds.

Mrs. T. J. Skiles.

LEMON-HONEY.

Beat four eggs to a cream, add to one cupful of sugar grated rind and juice of three lemons, butter the size of an egg; bring to a boil and add eggs, then boil five minutes stirring all the time.

Miss Hoge.

WHITE ICING.

One large cupful of granulated sugar, four tablespoonfuls boiling water, boil until waxy, pour over the beaten whites of three eggs and beat until cool.

Mrs. Swartz.

HONEY CAKES.

Rub one egg into one cupful of brown sugar, add one cup molasses; in three tablespoonfuls cold water stir one tablespoonful soda; add to the above; stir in flour to make a stiff batter, let it rise over night; in the morning stir in just flour enough to roll out like cookies.

Miss Hoge.

GOLD CAKE.

One cup sugar, one-half cup butter, two cups flour, one and a half teaspoonfuls Royal Baking Powder, one-half cup sweet milk, yolks of eight eggs.

Mrs. Swartz.

MARBLE CAKE.

White—One cup white sugar, one-half cup of butter, one-half cup sweet milk, two cups flour, two teaspoonfuls Royal Baking Powder, whites of four eggs. Black—One cup brown sugar, one-half cup molasses, one-half cup butter, one-half cup of sour milk, yolks of four eggs, one tablespoonful cinnamon, half a nutmeg, other spices to suit the taste, one teaspoonful soda, two and a half cupfuls of flour.

Mrs. Swartz.

DELICATE AND FRUIT CAKE.

Two cupfuls of sugar, three-fourths cupful of butter, two and a half cupfuls of flour, one cupful sweet milk, three teaspoonfuls Royal Baking Powder, whites of five eggs.

Fruit Lining for above—Take four tablespoonfuls of dough, one-half cupful of raisins, same of currants and citron, half a cupful of flour, half a cupful of molasses or white sugar, made into a syrup; bake in layers, two of which white with fruit layer in the middle. Put together with white icing.

Miss Hedges.

ORANGE CREAM FOR LAYER CAKE.

Put in a coffee cup the grated rind of one and juice of two large oranges, two tablespoonfuls of lemon juice, fill up with with water, strain and put on to boil, add one tablespoonful of corn starch, which has been wet with cold water; stir until thick, then cook over hot water for ten minutes; beat yolks of two eggs, add four tablespoonfuls sugar, stir into the above mixture, cook one minute, add two teaspoonfuls of butter. When cool spread between the layers of your cake.

Mrs. A. Letson.

WHITE POUND CAKE.

One cup pulverized sugar; and one-half cup butter, beaten to a cream, add the well-beaten whites of two eggs, and beat ten minutes; sift one teaspoonful cream of tartar and one-half teaspoonful soda through one and a half cupfuls of flour; stir flour in with half cupful of sweet milk, beat all together fifteen minutes. Bake from forty-five minutes to one hour. For a large cake truble the quantity.

Mrs. F. Damon.

SOFT GINGER BREAD.

Dissolve two level teaspoofuls soda in one cup boiling water, add to it one cup Orleans molasses, two-thirds cupful butter, two-thirds cupful brown sugar, two teaspoonfuls cinnamon, one of cloves, one of ginger, two cups flour; add last two well beaten eggs.

Mrs. F. Damon.

UNCOOKED ICING.

Whites of three eggs, three cups of confectioner's sugar, three tablespoonfuls lemon juice; put the eggs in a large bowl, sprinkle with three teaspoonfuls sugar, add three teaspoonfuls sugar every five minutes, beating all the time; when it begins to thicken add the lemon juice and beat as before. Do not use all the sugar unless needed.

Mrs. A. Letson.

WHITE CAKE.

One and a half cupfuls butter, two and a half cupfuls pulverized sugar, four cupfuls flour, whites of twelve eggs, juice of one lemon, half a teaspoonful of soda, mix soda in the flour and sift several times; beat butter to a cream and add flour very gradually until it is a smooth paste, beat the eggs to a stiff froth and mix in the sugar, stir eggs and sugar into the flour and butter, add lemon juice and mix smoothly. Be careful in mixing to follow directions exactly as given. MRS. A. LETSON.

GINGER SNAPS.

One pint of Orleans molasses and one cup of lard, boiled together; when cool add one tablespoonful of soda dissolved in a little cold water, one tablespoonful of ginger, a pinch of pepper, scant teaspoonful of salt, flour enough to thicken; roll out *very* thin and bake in a quick oven. MRS. A. LETSON.

PHILADELPHIA CAKE.

White part—One cupful of white sugar, one-half cupful of butter, one-half cupful of sweet milk, two teaspoonfuls of Royal baking powder, whites of four eggs, two cupfuls of flour.

Dark part—One cupful of brown sugar, one-half cupful of molasses, one-half cupful of butter, one-half cupful of sour milk, one tablespoonful of cinnamon, one teaspoonful of cloves, one-half nutmeg, one teaspoonful of soda, two and a half cupfuls of flour, one cupful of raisins, one of currants. Add figs and citron if you wish. Ice with white icing or lemon honey.

MISS HOGE.

WASHINGTON CAKE.

One cupful of boiling water, three cupfuls of brown sugar, one cupful of sweet milk, five eggs, one teaspoonful of cinnamon, one-half teaspoonful of cloves, nutmeg, one cupful of seeded raisins, two teaspoonfuls of Royal baking powder, three cupfuls of flour.

MRS. INNES.

FRUIT CAKE.

One and a half cupfuls of butter, three cupfuls of brown sugar, one cupful of molasses, one-half cupful of whisky, one-half cupful of sour milk, one small teaspoonful of soda, four eggs, three tablespoonfuls of cinnamon, one and a half of cloves, one of allspice, one-fourth of mace, one nutmeg, six and a half cupfuls of flour, five pounds of seeded raisins, two pounds of currants, one and a half pounds of citron. Mix butter and eggs together, add sour milk in which the soda has been stirred, spices, whisky and flour, leaving out enough flour to dredge fruit thoroughly; add fruit and molasses, put two layers of heavy brown paper in pan and bake four hours in moderate oven.

Miss Robinson.

MUSTARD CREAM CAKE.

One cupful of butter, two cupfuls of sugar, three cupfuls of flour, one cupful of sweet milk, four eggs, three teaspoonfuls of Royal baking powder.

Custard—Two tablespoonfuls of corn starch dissolved in a little cold milk, one-half pound of English walnuts broken in small pieces. Put in double boiler and cook until thick. Spread each layer of cake with sweet jelly, then custard; ice the cake with cooked icing; ornament with the small halves of the walnuts. Shell bark hickory nuts may be used in place of the walnuts.

Mrs. John Carlin.

OLD-FASHIONED POUND CAKE.

One pound of butter, one pound of sugar, one pound of flour, eight eggs, one-half teacupful of brandy or whisky, one half nutmeg grated, two teaspoonfuls of Royal baking powder. Beat butter, sugar and yolks of eggs until very light, then add flour, brandy, nutmeg, and whites of eggs. Bake in a moderate oven one hour.

Mrs. Robinson.

CRAWFORD & TAYLOR,

CRACKER AND CAKE BAKERS,

MANSFIELD, · OHIO.

Never before has there been such a splendid variety of goods offered to the people.

ASK YOUR GROCER FOR NONE OTHER.

CHASE & SANBORN'S SEAL BRAND COFFEE IS THE BEST.

A RARE BLEND OF PRIVATE PLANTATION JAVA AND ARABIAN MOCHA—GREAT STRENGTH— EXQUISITE FLAVOR—ABSOLUTE PURITY—UNIFORMITY AND RICHNESS.

CHARLES WENDT,
Sole Agent for Kenton.

CREAM PUFFS.

Pour one-half pint of boiling water over one scant teacupful of butter, stir until thoroughly dissolved, and while hot stir in two cupfuls of flour. When the whole is thoroughly scalded and *very* smooth, set away to cool; When cold break in five eggs, stir well, add one teaspoonful of Royal baking powder. Drop on buttered paper and bake. When cold, break open carefully and fill with the following cream.

Cream—One pint of milk, one-half cupful of flour, one cupful of sugar, stir all together and cook until as thick as cream. Flavor with lemon juice.

Miss Hoge.

SNOW-DRIFT CAKE.

One cupful of sweet milk, two cupfuls of sugar, one-half cupful of butter, three cupfuls of flour, whites of five eggs, two teaspoonfuls of Royal baking powder, one teaspoonful of lemon or vanilla. This can be baked as a solid cake or in layers.

Mrs. Russell.

FIG CAKE.

Two cupfuls of confectioners sugar, one cupful of butter, one cupful of sweet milk, whites of ten eggs beaten to a froth, two teaspoonfuls of Royal baking powder, two teaspoonfuls of vanilla, four cupfuls of sifted flour.

Fig filling.—One and a half pounds of figs chopped, one pound of seeded raisins, two cupfuls of sugar, with water enough to cover, boiled to a taffy, whites of four eggs beaten and stir in sugar while hot, beat until light. Put chopped raisins and figs between layers and then pour frosting over them. Ice the top with frosting alone.

Mrs. A. W. Janes.

GINGER CRACKERS.

One and one-half pounds flour, one-fourth pound butter, one-fourth pound lard, one-half pound brown sugar, two tablespoonfuls of ginger, one nutmeg, one-half ounce cinnamon, one-half cupful sour milk in which dissolve one-half teaspoonful soda, two eggs, thoroughly mix flour and spices, then eggs and milk, then use molasses enough to make a stiff dough. Roll thin and bake in a slack oven. To work on the board without sticking, boil lard, butter and molasses for a short time, allowing it to become cold before using. Put your crackers in a cotton bag and hang up in a warm room to keep them hard and crisp.

Mrs. Garrettson.

SPONGE CAKE.

Two cupfuls of sugar, (powdered makes the smoothest cake) two cupfuls of flour, four eggs, half cupful hot water, one teaspoonful Royal baking powder. Beat yolks light, add sugar, then flour and beaten whites gradually, sifting baking powder with last half cupful of flour; when well mixed stir in quickly the hot water, and bake in a moderate oven forty minutes.

Miss Berrall.

LEMON CREAM.

Two lemons grated (entire), one coffee cupful of sugar (white) two eggs beaten well together, add one tablespoonful melted butter and let all stand in a vessel placed in boiling water. Let it stand till cool. Is best with plain one, two, three, four, cake.

Miss Halliday.

SOFT GINGERBREAD.

One cupful molasses, one cupful sugar, three cupfuls flour, one-half cupful sour milk, one-half cupful melted lard, one egg, one teaspoonful soda, two teaspoonfuls ginger.

Miss Spelman.

COLUMBIA CAKE.

One cupful of butter, two cupfuls of brown sugar, one cupful of milk, three cupfuls of flour, one cupful of seeded raisins, one teaspoonful of cinnamon, half a teaspoonful of allspice, half a teaspoonful of grated nutmeg, two teaspoonfuls of Royal baking powder. Bake in two layers, ice with white icing.

Miss Hoge.

MACAROONS.

Blanch a pound of almonds, rub to a paste; beat the whites of three eggs to a stiff froth, stir in gradually half a pound of pulverized sugar and the almond paste. Drop small spoonfuls on buttered paper, sift sugar over them, and bake slowly. Can flavor with vanilla, or rose extract if desired.

Miss Hoge.

BEVERAGES.

COFFEE.

The best coffee is made by mixing two-thirds Java and one-third Mocha. Coffee should be carefully and evenly roasted, not a berry being allowed to burn. Coffee is best the first day it is roasted. Allow a *heaping* tablespoonful of coffee and a cup of *boiling* water for each person, also a heaping tablespoonful of coffee and a cup of boiling water for the pot. Settle with the white of an egg, a tiny pinch of salt, and wet with a little cold water; beat thoroughly, then add the boiling water. Boil ten minutes, set back where it will keep hot, but not boil, ten minutes more.

Miss Hoge.

TEA.

The most desirable tea is Formosa Oolong. Use none but earthen or china tea pots; those with inside strainers being best. The water must be absolutely *boiling* when poured upon the leaves. Allow an even teaspoonful of tea to each person. Put the tea in the strainer and pour the boiling water slowly upon it. To obtain the finest flavor, serve in one minute; if allowed to stand the aroma will be lost. Connoisseurs do not use cream. Russian tea is made in the same manner, only adding a slice of lemon to each cup. Of course no cream.

Mr. Robert S. Innes.

CHOCOLATE.

To one quart of rich milk add twelve tablespoonfuls of grated chocolate. Bring your milk to a boil; rub the chocolate smooth with a little cold milk; add to the milk. Beat the white of an egg with half a teacupful of sugar; add to the milk and chocolate. Flavor with vanilla. Boil an hour, two hours won't hurt; add more cream if desired. Serve with with whipped cream.

Miss Hoge.

COCOA.

Cocoa has the same flavor as chocolate, but is richer and more oily. It is prepared the same as chocolate.

GEORGE WASHINGTON EGG-NOG.

Three quarts of milk, one quart of brandy or whiskey, one dozen of eggs, one and one-fourth pounds of finely powdered sugar, flavor it with Jamaica or Santa Cruz Rum, say two-thirds of a tumbler or full tumbler. Mix sugar and yolks to a cream, add whiskey, whites beaten stiff, milk and rum. Make and use the same day. The liquor must be of the best quality, the milk new, and the eggs fresh.

This receipt was given to General Robinson by Mr. L. Q. Washington, a descendant of General Washington.

LEMONADE.

Rub loaf sugar over the rind of the lemon to absorb the oil, add to the lemon juice the sugar to taste. Two lemons will make three glassfuls of lemonade, the remainder of the ingredients being water and plenty of chopped ice.

CLARET PUNCH.

One bottle of claret, one-fourth the quantity of ice water, three lemons sliced, three-fourths of a cup of powdered sugar. Cover the sliced lemon with sugar, and let it stand ten minutes; add water, stir hard, and pour in the wine. Put pounded ice into each glass before filling with the mixture.

Mrs. Newlon.

BLACKBERRY CORDIAL WITH BRANDY.

One quart of blackberry juice, three-fourths of a pound of white sugar, half an ounce each of grated nutmeg and powdered cinnamon, one-fourth ounce each of allspice and cloves, one pint of French brandy. Tie the spices in thin muslin bags. Boil juice, sugar, and spices together fifteen minutes, skimming well; add the brandy, set aside in a closely covered vessel to cool. When cold, strain out the spices, and bottle, sealing the corks.

BLACKBERRY CORDIAL WITHOUT BRANDY.

Mash the berries, cover with water and let stand until the pulp rises to the top and forms a crust; this will take about three days. Draw off the fluid into another vessel, and to every gallon of juice add one pound of sugar. Stir well every day for ten days, then for every gallon of juice add one quart of water, and to every quarter of a gallon of juice (measured before adding water) one pound of crushed sugar. Set on the stove, and let come to a boil; when the scum rises, skim and bottle at once. This is good as soon as cold, but will keep for years and improve with age.

Mrs. W. S. Robinson.

MILK PUNCH.

Take sweet rich milk, and sweeten to taste, and add one to two tablespoonfuls of best brandy, add pounded ice, and shake. This is for one glassful.

Mrs. S. L. Hoge.

RASPBERRY VINEGAR.

Fill a two gallon jar half full of fresh raspberries, cover them with the best white sugar; let it stand four days, strain carefully, fill the jar again and with fresh fruit, pouring the liquor over it; let stand four days longer, then strain the vinegar through a jelly bag. Weigh the juice and take the same weight in sugar, boil a few minutes, remove the scum; when cold, bottle. This syrup mixed with water and ice is very refreshing.

PRESERVING.

Care must be taken that the fruit is fresh and firm. White crushed sugar is best to use, but granulated sugar will do very well. Always make a rich syrup before putting fruit in. Cook fruit until tender, take from syrup, and then cook syrup until very rich and drop fruit in for a few moments. The rule is one pound of sugar to one pound of fruit and half a pint of water. To clarify the syrup, put over the fire and before it becomes hot mix into it the well beaten white of an egg. When it begins to boil remove scum as it rises, and be careful that it does not boil over. Let boil until no more scum rises. When the fruit is ready for the cans take from the kettle and place in the jars carefully in order not to break the fruit, then fill up the jar with the hot syrup and seal. This rule for preserving will answer for peaches, pears, plums and all other fruits.

CITRON PRESERVES.

The citron can be pared, cored and sliced, or cut into fancy shapes with cutters which are made for the purpose. Put the citron in a preserving kettle and cover with strong alum water, and boil half an hour or until clear, then drain and let stand in cold water over night. In the morning drain and weigh, being careful to see that all the seeds have been removed, take an equal quantity of sugar. Take two quarts of water to six pounds of fruit, and equal quantity of sugar, and one-half pound of white ginger root and boil for a few minutes, then add sugar and let cook until a rich syrup, then add fruit and cook until tender and transparent, take from the kettle and cook the syrup until it is very rich and thick, then drop the fruit in for a few moments to get hot through. You can add slices of lemon if you wish.

Miss Robinson.

YELLOW TOMATO PRESERVES.

Choose little plum-shaped tomatoes. Peel and prick them with a large needle, weigh tomatoes and to each pound of fruit take a pound of sugar and small cup of water; put sugar and water in preserving kettle and let dissolve slowly; boil until rich and put in tomatoes, when clear take out and place on platters for an hour. Put syrup on stove at the end of an hour, and clarify with the well beaten white of an egg, boil and *skim well;* then add the lemon sliced thin (one lemon to three pounds of fruit), let boil until very rich and drop in the tomatoes, cook a few moments and can. If the tomatoes are too ripe they will break up.

Miss Robinson.

RULE FOR MAKING JAM.

Mash fruit, put in preserving kettle and let *boil* fifteen minutes, stirring all the time; then add sugar, pint for pint, and let it boil five minutes. This way gives the fruit a more delicate flavor.

PRESERVED STRAWBERRIES.

Take a pound of sugar to a pound of fruit, and half a cup of water to each pound of sugar; boil the sugar and water to a rich syrup, drop in the fruit and boil until the fruit becomes transparent, skim out the fruit carefully, lay on platters; boil syrup down until very rich, drop in the fruit until hot through, pour into glass jars, and seal. Wrap your jars in paper and keep in a cool dark place.

MISS HOGE.

BRANDY PEACHES.

Select large, fine peaches; make a syrup, taking a pound of sugar to each pound of fruit, with small cup of water; clarify it, and when the syrup is rich drop in the fruit and cook until tender and clear; then take from kettle and cook syrup until very rich, drop fruit in for a moment; fill jars with fruit, and fill half full with syrup, then add best French brandy to top of can. Seal jars carefully.

TO JELLY FRUITS.

Free the fruit from all blemishes and put into a porcelain preserving kettle with only enough clear water to keep them from burning. Let boil until soft, then strain through flannel jelly bag and then through a cotton bag; return juice to clean kettle and boil from ten to fifteen minutes, then add sugar, to a pound of juice one pound of sugar, and let boil from three to five minutes, then turn into mould and stand until cold before covering. This rule will do for all jellies.

CURRANT JELLY.

Take ripe currants, mash, put over the fire in a porcelain kettle, letting them thoroughly scald, and strain through a jelly bag; for each pint of juice add one pint of white sugar, boil the juice fifteen minutes, skimming well, then stir in the sugar as you would for corn meal mush. It is better to have the sugar in a bright pan in the oven a few minutes before using so that it will not cool the juice. After the sugar is added cook until it boils, when it will be done.

BLACKBERRY JELLY.

Is made after receipt for currant jelly, but be careful not to make too stiff, as it grows thicker standing.

RULE FOR MARMALADE.

Mash the fruit, put in a preserving kettle, add the sugar, to a pound of fruit one pound of sugar, and boil from three-fourths to one hour, stirring constantly.

RED RASPBERRY JAM.

Three-fourths of a pound of sugar to one pound of fruit, one pint of currant juice to four pounds of fruit; boil the currant juice and raspberries together, mash and stir well, add sugar, and cook twenty minutes longer.

Strawberries and blackberries can be made into jam in the same manner, only omitting the currant juice.

Miss Hoge.

SPICED PEACHES.

Twelve pounds of fruit, six pounds of sugar, one-half pint of vinegar, spices to suit taste.

Mrs. Thomson.

SPICED PEACHES.

To nine pounds of fruit add three pounds of sugar, one pint of vinegar, spices to taste. Boil sugar and vinegar, add spices (stick cinnamon and whole cloves, and mace if you like), which must be tied up in thin muslin bags; put in the fruit and cook a few minutes, take out carefully and place in a stone jar, pour the syrup over them; for five mornings drain off the syrup, heat, and pour over the fruit; the last morning cook the syrup until as rich as you wish, pour over the fruit, and cover the jar tightly, first with muslin, then a layer of cotton batting, then heavy paper. If the peaches are soft do not cook them, simply pour over them the hot syrup.

Miss Hoge.

FOR SWEET PICKLES.

ANY FRUIT.—Eight pounds of fruit, three pounds of sugar, one quart of vinegar, spices, cinnamon. cloves, one small teaspoonful each. Stew fruit till tender. Boil sugar and vinegar, with spices, to a rich syrup and pour over when cool.

FOR CUCUMBERS.—Same syrup, boiled only ten minutes, poured when cold over cucumbers previously soaked in salt water one night.
MRS. THOMSON.

SPICED PEARS.

If the pears are hard, steam until tender, pour over the syrup the same as for spiced peaches. If Bartlett pears are used they are soft and do not need cooking.
MISS HOGE.

SPICED CHERRIES.

Stone the cherries, make a syrup as for peaches, and pour over for five mornings in the same manner.
MISS HOGE.

WATER MELON PICKLES.

Select a water melon with a thick rind and cut in large slices, taking out the soft center and all that is pink; pare the green rind from the firm white portion of the melon, and cut into such shape as you choose, put in preserving kettle and cover with strong alum water, let boil until tender enough to run a straw through, then drain and throw in cold water and let stand over night. In the morning take in hand and squeeze all the water from each slice, put in a jar and pour syrup over. One quart of vinegar, three pints of sugar, two ounces of cloves, and two ounces of stick cinnamon, make this into a syrup and pour over melon, scalding hot, six mornings. When the pickles have stood some time they are richer.
MISS ROBINSON.

MARYLAND PEACH PICKLE.

Pour boiling water over cling peaches, then wipe dry, put into kettle of hot water, boil until able to penetrate with a straw; have your syrup ready in another kettle, pour the peaches in, boil fifteen minutes, then put in air-tight glass jars. To make the syrup, three pounds of sugar and one pint of vinegar to a peck of peaches. This will be found a most delicious accompaniment to cold meats.

Mrs. Garretson.

PEACHES CANNED IN SUGAR AND VINEGAR.

Take nice large peaches, either cling or free stones, throw a few at a time into boiling water for a minute or two, take out and rub off the skin; take one and a half pints of sugar, and one-half pint of vinegar, stir well together and boil until clear, then drop in peaches enough for one can; cook slowly for about ten minutes, put in a glass jar, fill up with the syrup and seal. If there is a little syrup left add more eggs and vinegar for another can. Twelve or thirteen whole peaches will fill a one-quart jar.

PICKLES.

BORDEAUX SAUCE.

Two gallons of cabbage cut fine, one gallon of green tomatoes chopped, one dozen onions chopped, one ounce of celery seed, one ounce of ground allspice, one ounce of black pepper, one of cloves and one of ginger, one-half pound of white mustard seed, three-fourths gill of salt, three-fourths pound of sugar, one gallon good vinegar. Mix well and boil fifteen to twenty minutes. Horse radish and cauliflower make it better. You can add five cents worth of turmeric powder if you wish.

Mrs. Shingle.

SLICED CUCUMBERS.

Slice two dozen cucumbers with eight onions; salt them for a few hours and then put in colander and press out all the water; mix one tablespoonful of white pepper, one of mustard, one of turmeric powder and one small teacup of sugar. Mix with cucumbers and onions, add vinegar enough to cover all and cook thirty minutes. Put in glass jars and seal.

Mrs. Robinson.

AX JAR PICKLES.

Take a variety of young fruit and vegetables; put in strong salt water, let stand two or three days or until salty enough. Then put in cold water; wash carefully and let all the water drain off. Then to a three gallon jar add one-half pound of sliced horse radish, one hundred small onions, two ounces of mace, one ounce of cloves, two nutmegs, two pounds of crushed sugar, one-half bottle of ground mustard, one-half pound of yellow mustard seed, one-half pound of ginger root and almost one-half pound of turmeric powder stirred up with enough cold water to liquefy. Pour this over the pickles, then take enough good cider vinegar to cover all, boil and skim, pour over while boiling hot. Good to use in a week.

Mrs. Mac Connell.

CUCUMBER PICKLES.

Pour boiling water over the pickles, when cold, drain, sprinkle dry salt (one-half pint to one hundred pickles) over them; cover again with boiling water; for seven mornings, drain off this brine, bring to a boiling point, and pour over the pickles; while in this brine cover well with grape leaves; then draw from the brine, cover with weak vinegar and keep hot (without boiling) for five or six hours, then wipe dry and put in jars; then prepare your vinegar—to every gallon of vinegar add two pounds of brown sugar, one pound of black mustard seed, half an ounce of allspice, mace, celery seed, horse radish, red pepper, black pepper, cinnamon and a few small onions if you wish.

Miss Hoge.

EAST INDIA PICKLES

Take enough small heads of cabbage and cauliflower to fill a three gallon jar. Pour over them a strong brine of salt and water; keep well covered with brine two weeks; then take out of jar, and lay in cold water for two or three hours. (After removing the cauliflower from the brine, boil until tender.) Cucumbers and small onions may be used instead of cabbage, they must be put in pickle for three or four days, and then drained, and the following mixture poured over. One-fourth pound each of whole black pepper, allspice, cloves; one-half pound of ground mustard, one gallon of white wine vinegar, four pounds of sugar, one pound of *white* mustard seed and one of *black*, one-fourth pound of celery seed, mace to suit taste, a little horse radish, two ounces of turmeric. Tie part of the spices in thin muslin bags, mix mustard and turmeric smooth with vinegar.

Dr. Walton.

CUCUMBER SALAD.

One dozen sliced cucumbers, three good sized onions sliced, salt as for table; let stand four hours and pour off salt water. One pint of vinegar, one cup of white sugar, one teaspoonful each of ground white pepper, mustard, ginger and one of grain mustard, one of stick cinnamon. Boil hard fifteen minutes.

Mrs. Shingle.

CATSUP.

One bushel of tomatoes, two quarts of vinegar, one-half pound of whole black pepper, the same of allspice and cloves, two ounces of ground mustard, twelve good sized onions, three pounds of sugar, two handfuls of peach leaves; boil three hours, stirring often. Put onions, cloves, allspice and pepper, with the tomatoes at first. Put in the mustard while cooking before straining; after it is strained, add the vinegar and a little cayenne pepper. Boil until thick as desired (about two hours).

Mrs. Hoge.

SWEET TOMATO CATSUP.

To eighteen pounds of tomatoes, after having been put through the sieve, take eight pounds of sugar, one quart of vinegar, more if desired, three tablespoonfuls of pepper, three tablespoonfuls of salt, three tablespoonfuls of ginger, three tablespoonfuls of cloves, eight tablespoonfuls of cinnamon. Cook to proper consistency.

Mrs. Thomson.

TOMATO CATSUP.

To one-half bushel of ripe tomatoes, (it is best to skin them) add one small handful of peach leaves, six chopped onions, one-half ounce of whole cloves. Boil these together until the tomatoes are well cooked; rub through a sieve fine enough to retain the seeds. Boil down until quite thick, stirring all the time to keep from burning; then add two quarts of strong cider vinegar, one ounce ground allspice, one nutmeg, one pint of light brown sugar, one-half teacupful of salt, one ounce of ground mustard, one-half ounce of ground black pepper, one ounce of cinnamon, one drachm of cayenne pepper. Boil half an hour after the spices are in. If you want red catsup leave out the dark spices.

Mrs. Philips.

CANDIES.

BUTTER SCOTCH.

One cup of brown sugar, one half cup of water, one teaspoonful of vinegar, piece of butter size of a walnut. Boil twenty minutes. Flavor if desired.

CHOCOLATE.

Mold the cream into cone shape and with a fork dip into melted chocolate, using Fry's chocolate.

Miss Shingle.

CREAM CANDY.

Two cupfuls of sugar and one-half cupful of milk stirred together. When dissolved, boil ten minutes. Take from fire and beat to a cream, flavor to taste. Add chopped nuts if you wish.

Mrs. Swartz.

ICE CREAM CANDY.

Three cups of white sugar; one-half cup of vinegar; one-half cup of water; butter size of an egg. Boil until it will harden when dipped in cold water. Pour on buttered plates, when cold enough to handle, pull until white, then cut into sticks. Do not stir while boiling.

Mrs. Swartz.

CHOCOLATE CREAMS.

To one quart of water, one and a half tablespoonfuls of arrowroot, and two cups of sugar. Boil eight minutes, add one teaspoonful of vanilla. Take off the stove, beat it fifteen minutes, or until it creams. Melt one-half sack of Fry's chocolate and roll the creams in it.

ORANGE DROPS.

Grate the rind of one orange and squeeze the juice taking care to reject the seeds; add to this a pinch of tartaric acid, then stir in confectioners' sugar until it is stiff enough to form into small balls the size of small marble. Lemon juice can be used instead of orange, then leave out the tartaric acid.

Miss Robinson.

FRENCH VANILLA CREAN.

Break into a bowl the white of one or more eggs, as the quantity you wish to make will require, add to it an equal quantity of cold water, then stir in confectioners' sugar until you have it stiff enough to mould into shape with the fingers; flavor with vanilla. This is the foundation for all French creams. Add any kind of fruits or nuts, form into shapes and lay on buttered plates.

Miss Shingl.

COCOANUT BALLS.

Mix the cream not quite so stiff as for other candies, then mix the cocoanut thoroughly through the cream and mould into balls.

Dates filled with cream make a very pretty and nice candy.

English walnuts, almonds and figs can be used in many different ways.

MOLASSES CANDY.

One quart of molasses; one-half cup of butter, one-half cup of sugar. Boil fast, and when done stir in half a teaspoonful of soda just before taking from the fire.

MISS HEDGES.

MISCELLANEOUS.

SALTED ALMONDS.

Blanch one cupful of almonds. When cold put one tablespoonful of salad oil or melted butter on the almonds and let stand one hour, then sprinkle with one tablespoonful of salt. Put them into a bright baking pan in a moderate oven, and cook them with an occasional stirring, until they are a delicate brown, about twenty minutes. Peanuts can be treated in the same way.

MISS ROBINSON.

TO BLANCH ALMONDS.

Shell the nuts, pour boiling water over them; let them stand in the water a minute, and then throw them into cold water. Rub between the hands.

ZEST.

Rub loaf sugar over the surface of the lemon or orange. The friction breaks the oil-ducts, and the sugar absorbs the oil. The sugar should then be pounded fine, or it can be melted.

The Cook's Table of Weights and Measures.

1 quart of sifted flour equals 1 lb.
1 quart of powdered sugar equals 1 lb. 7 oz.
1 quart of granulated sugar equals 1 lb. 9 oz.
1 pint of closely packed butter equals 1 lb.
Butter size of an egg equals about 2 oz.
10 eggs equal 1 lb.
3 cupfuls of sugar equal 1 lb.
5 cupfuls of sifted flour equal 1 lb.
1 heaping tablespoonful equals 1-6 gill.
4 gills equal 1 pint.
2 pints equal 1 quart.
4 quarts equal 1 gallon.

TO CHOP SUET.

Sprinkle flour over it while chopping, which will prevent the pieces from adhering.

TO SEED RAISINS.

Sprinkle flour over the raisins, or pour boiling water over them when seeding.

TO MAKE ROUX.

Roux is a mixture of flour and butter *cooked*. It is better for soups and sauces when cooked. When the butter is brought to the boiling point, the sifted flour is sprinkled in; mix well over the fire until the flour is well cooked.

Parsley and mint can be dried and kept for use.

MADE MUSTARD.

Half a pound of mustard; pour boiling water on it until you can rub smooth; add one teaspoonful of salt, one tablespoonful each of sugar, and of melted butter or olive oil. Thin with vinegar.

Mrs. Robinson.

TO CRSYTALIZE FRUIT.

Make a syrup of sugar and water, boil until clear and waxy, dip in Malaga grapes, segments of oranges, or fresh strawberries. Keep in a cold place.

Miss Hoge.

CHEESE STRAWS.

The following is said to be a genuine, original recipe for the cheese straws that are now a fashionable delicacy at dinner parties: take two ounces of the best pastry flour, and mix in a little pepper and salt, together with just a dust of cayenne pepper, rub in two ounces of butter, as for pie crust, and when these are thoroughly incorporated, add two ounces of grated cheese, (Parmesan, preferably, but any dry, strong sort will do). Work the mixture to a smooth paste with the yolk of an egg; should there not be sufficient moisture in the yolk of one egg, use part of another or a very little lemon juice, but on no account add water, which has a tendency to make the paste tough. Work the paste until it is smooth and stiff, and roll it out until about an eighth of an inch thick, then cut into straws about five inches long and a quarter of an inch wide.

SOUTH AMERICAN MARMALADE.

Take one dozen sour oranges. Cut the rind into quarters and peel off; scrape all the white from the rind, cover with cold water and boil till tender. Scrape the skin and seeds from inner pulp; when the rind is tender, cut into thin shreds and mix with juice and pulp. Add to each pint of the mixture, one pound of granulated sugar. Boil steadily thirty minutes.

Mrs. Ryder.

CORNED BEEF.

To one hundred pounds of beef, four and a half pounds of salt, four gallons of water, two and a half pounds of brown sugar, one ounce of saltpetre. Boil and skim; when perfectly cool, pour carefully over the meat.

Mrs. Russell.

FOR CURING HAM.

Eight pounds of salt, two pounds of brown sugar, three ounces of soda, two ounces of saltpetre. Make brine and pour over the meat. This amount is for one hundred pounds of meat.

TO KEEP CIDER.

Place your barrel on the side, bung-hole at the top; make a bag of a piece of unbleached muslin half a yard long and two inches wide; push the bag through the hole and pour into it, with a funnel, eight ounces of powdered mustard, two ounces of prepared chalk, and two ounces of salt This is sufficient for forty gallons of cider, and should be kept tightly closed. Rack off cider, into clean barrel before adding mixture.

MR. SNYDER.

THINGS WORTH KNOWING.

Disinfectant.—Five gallons of rain water, one-eighth ounce nitrate of lead, one-half ounce of common salt. Mix thoroughly. Good and cheap. MR. FRED DAY.

Furniture Polish.—Take equal parts of olive oil, turpentine and vinegar. Apply with woolen cloth. MRS. SNYDER.

Floor Polish.—To a pint of linseed oil, pint of turpentine, and generous half pound of parafine melted with the oil, when removed from the fire add turpentine. This is rubbed at once upon the floor with woolen cloths and polished with woolen cloths or brush. In cold weather set the pan in a pail of hot water. Wash or destroy the cloths that are used as they are combustible.

MRS. H. O. H.

Furniture Wash.—One third each of alcohol or ammonia, turpentine and linseed oil. Apply with flannel cloth and polish with dry flannel.   Mrs. Shingle.

Furniture Wash.—One and a half ounces of alcohol, one-half ounce of muriatic acid eight ounces of linseed oil, one-half pint of the best vinegar, one and a half ounces of butter of antimony. Mix, putting in vinegar last. Apply with flannel cloth and polish with dry flannel.   Mrs. Shingle.

Stove Polish.—One pint of asphaltum, one quart of turpentine, one ounce tincture of benzine. Mix with stove polish.
   Mrs. Shingle.

Kettles are cleansed of onion and other odors by dissolving a teaspoonful of pearlash or saleratus in water and washing them with it.

If you put a piece of bread on the top of your knife when peeling onions, they will not affect your eyes, or if you peel onions under water your eyes will not cry.

To remove grass stains from white goods, wet with water, rub in some soft soap and as much baking soda as will adhere, let stand half an hour, wash out in the usual manner and the stain will be gone.

Put camphor gum with your silver ware, and it will never tarnish as long as the gum is there.

To drive away the little red ants sprinkle borax on the shelves.

Rub kerosene over rusted stoves once or twice during the summer.

To remove grease spots, rub magnesia on the spots, cover with two thicknesses of brown or blotting paper and apply a warm iron.

If an egg is clear and golden in appearance when held to the light it is good, if dark or spotted it is bad.

If the saucepan in which milk is to be boiled, should first be moistened with water it will prevent the milk from burning.

To clean paint dip a flannel cloth into warm soapsuds, then in powdered whiting, rub off the paint and rinse with clean water.

To remove paint from window frames, dissolve soda in hot water, wash the glass with it, and in half an hour rub the paint off with a dry cloth.

Beat carpets on the wrong side first, then on the right, after which spots may be removed with a tablespoonful of ammonia in a quart of warm soft water.

Iron rust can be removed from clothes by rubbing with lemon juice and laying in the sun.

To clean bottles, put into them fine coals, shake well either with or without water. Charcoal left in a bottle for a little time will take away disagreeable odors.

To polish tin use whiting which has been moistened with ammonia.

Brass Polish.—Rotten stone moistened with turpentine and applied with a flannel cloth will brighten brass quickly, rub briskly.

To clean straw matting, wash with weak salt water.

To remove rust from stove or pipe, rub over with a very little linseed oil. Build a slow fire in it to dry, then blacken with good polish.

Hartshorn will restore colors taken out by acids.

Sunshine on mirrors will injure their lustre, therefore do not hang opposite a door or window.

To remove blood stains, they can be removed from an article you do not care to wash by applying a thick paste of starch and cold water. Place in the sun and rub off in two hours; if the stain has not entirely disappeared, repeat the process.

A piece of dry bread put into a small bag and placed in the middle of your stewpan, in which onions or cabbage are being boiled, will absorb the strong flavor.

To remove ink from carpets, absorb as much as possible with a cloth, cover the spot thickly with salt, in a day or two the stain will disappear.

To Mend China.—This is a very old English receipt: Take a very thick solution of gum arabic in water and stir into it plaster of paris until the mixture becomes of the proper consistency. Apply it with a brush to the fractured edges of the china and stick them together. In three days the articles cannot be broken in the same place.

DINNER-GIVING.

A Few Suggestions on Dinner-Giving.

Small cheer and great welcome makes a merry feast.
—*Comedy of Errors.*

—All human history attests
That happiness for man—the hungry sinner—
Since Eve ate apples, must depend on dinners!
—*Don Juan.*

Invitations for very formal dinners are sent one to two weeks in advance, for informal dinners any time within a week is usually customary.

Invitations should be answered as soon as they are received. After having accepted a dinner invitation, let nothing interfere with your going except illness, and when that is the case, send an immediate note to the hostess that she may fill your place.

The hours generally selected for dinners are six, seven, and eight o'clock. Extreme punctuality on these occasions is to be observed. A hostess is never required to wait over fifteen minutes for a tardy guest.

One should always remember that a ceremonious dinner is the highest social compliment and should be met in a formal manner. When inviting friends who are visitors in a household where you have but slight acquaintance always include some member or members of the family in your invitations.

Visits should be made soon after a dinner party by all who have been invited whether the invitation was accepted or declined. It is a subject for consideration in selecting guests for a dinner party, as one is always anxious to throw agreeable and congenial people together. Good talkers are an important feature, as the charm of an otherwise successful dinner has been destroyed by dragging.

A great deal depends on the seating of the guests. In the hall should be a tray of cards with the name of gentlemen and the lady whom he is to take in to dinner. On entering the drawing room the lady precedes, *not* taking her husband's arm. After the arrival of the last guest, dinner should be announced, the host leading the way with the lady who is the honored guest, seating her on his right, the hostess following last, with the gentleman she wishes to honor, who is seated on her right. Each season brings its changes in the arrangement of dinner tables so there is no uniform style.

A thick baize or cotton flannel under the table cloth (for all meals) is a necessity, it prevents noise, the finest table linen looking comparatively thin without its use. Do not starch napkins. Table damask should be white and perfectly fresh, colored linen is permissible only for breakfast and tea. Flowers are usually the chief decoration of the table; the most artistic effect obtained is in employing one color; flowers out of season are a costly luxury, as lilies of the valley in October and clover in January.

The flat basket of flowers is not now popular, the high designs in cut glass and china are preferred. Low cut glass dishes for *bon bons* and candied fruits, china or glass candle-sticks with colored shades for candles are the usual decorations.

It is a very pretty welcome to see a bunch of flowers at each lady's plate, a *boutonniere* for the gentlemen; with these, dinner favors are frequently given, simple or very costly according to one's purse. Chairs should be of equal height at the table.

Avoid crowding guests, it destroys comfort and detracts from the enjoyment. Water and wine glasses should be carefully observed by servants, so as to be refilled as required, but the over filling of them should be carefully avoided. One is at liberty to refuse a dish passed, and any course that is placed before you.

Service *a la Russe*, is to prepare each course out of sight of the guests. This may be done by the servants handing each course previously arranged at side tables. Nothing is seen upon the dinner table except silver, glass and decorations. In this method of serving a dinner, vegetables or any accompaniment of a course are never to be passed from guest to guest, but should be put upon the plate before hand and then placed before the guest. The exceptions to this rule are in the serving of dessert, ices or creams, with cake. The latter are handed to guests as soon as the course is placed before them, and are afterwards placed upon the dinner table.

Servants begin passing dishes to the guest at the right hand of host, each one being served in turn, no distinction being made further than at commencement. For each course the servants should place a plate before each guest. The tray is held low for the convenience of the guests in helping themselves to what is passed. If there is but one servant in waiting the silver on each plate after a course should be removed first as it saves time. Care should be taken that servants move as noiselessly as possible, unnecessary noise in handling silver and glass to be avoided. Servants should never seem to notice the conversation of people at the table. No accident at table should disturb the lady of the house. If her rare china and glass should be broken before her she must not seem to be aware of it, as unconsciously her feelings are communicated to her guests. All directions about serving should be explicitly explained before hand, so that unnecessary interchange of looks and words between mistress and servants may be avoided. Written directions for the order of courses (for any formal meal) should be tacked up in kitchen and pantry. Some waiting maids are as thoroughly trained as butler or footman. A mistress of a house should always be capable of teaching her servants how to lay a table and wait upon it properly. Where there is only a maid servant for waiting the mistress makes all necessary arrangements. In a wealthy family one will find a butler and footman. In this country frequently a footman is erroneously called waiter, the latter being the name for a hotel dining room servant—not a private one.

Menus should be provided for elaborate dinners, one being placed by each plate. Guests are thus enabled to partake more or less freely of dishes *chacun à son goùt.* Menus are of many fanciful and unique designs. It is perfectly proper for them to be taken by guests upon leaving the table as mementos of the occasion. The hostess gives the signal for leaving the table, the guests passing from the dining room in the order they are seated, without precedence. The wish that the gentlemen should remain at the table to smoke is shown by the cigars being handed whilst guests are at the dinner table, otherwise the host provides cigars in his library or smoking room.

Never play with food or handle unnecessarily the glass and silver at your plate.

Flowers should not be put upon the table long before dinner is served as they are apt to be wilted by the heat.

A *carafe* should be put on the table fresh from the ice chest.

When a lady removes her gloves for a dinner it should be done as soon as she is seated. One of the latest fashions for very ceremonious dinners is *not* to remove the gloves.

MENUS.

MENUS FOR BREAKFAST.

The hours for a formal breakfast are from nine to twelve o'clock.

SPRING.

Sliced Oranges.
Broiled Shad; Sliced Cucumbers.
Saratoga Potatoes.
Fried Chicken; Cream Sauce.
French Peas.
Omelet; Radishes.
Rolls.
Waffles; Maple Syrup.
Tea; Coffee.

SUMMER.

Strawberries.
Stewed Sweet breads; Cream Sauce.
Minced Potatoes with Parsley.
Broiled Chicken.
Green Peas; Rolls.
Frozen Peaches; Whipped Cream.
Tea; Coffee.

FALL.

Nutmeg Melon.
Fried Oysters; Celery Sauce.
Rolls.
Broiled Tenderloin Steak.

Mushroom Sauce.
Fried Sweet Potatoes; Muffins.
French Omelet; Buttered Toast.
Rice Griddle Cakes; Maple Syrup.
Tea; Coffee.

WINTER.

Baked Apples; Whipped Cream.
Fried Smelts; Tartar Sauce.
Milk Biscuit.
Breaded Mutton Chops.
Tomato Sauce.
Escaloped Potatoes; Drop Biscuit.
Eggs in Paper Cases; French Toast.
Buckwheat Cakes; Maple Syrup.
Chocolate; Coffee:

LUNCHEON.

The hours for a formal lunch are from one until half past two o'clock.

Oysters on the Half Shell.
Bouillon.
Baked Crabs.
Stewed Sweet breads; Green Peas.
Maryland Biscuit.
Chocolate.
Claret Punch in Lemon Skins.
Chicken Croquettes; Cream Potatoes.
Quick Biscuit; Currant Jelly.
Oyster Pate.
Celery Salad; Cheese Sandwiches.
Olives.
Frozen Apricots; Cake.
Fruit; Nuts; Coffee.

—— Ask your Grocer for the famous ——

"GOLDEN FLEECE" FLOUR.

This flour needs no recommendation other than that thousands of families use it daily. If your grocer has not a supply he may obtain it from the mill for you. We guarantee sweet, white, moist bread all the year round.

WARDER & BARNETT,
SPRINGFIELD, OHIO.

CHARLES WENDT,
Agent for "Golden Fleece," KENTON, OHIO.

REFINED CORN STARCH,
FOR FOOD PURPOSES,
—— Made by ——

GEORGE FOX STARCH COMPANY,
CINCINNATI, OHIO.
—— Is ——

ABSOLUTELY PURE.

Use no other. See that the "Fox's Head" is on every package, as there are many imitations of this famous starch.

A house which stands as it were in the street, which is not separated either by a hedge or fence from the public thoroughfare, is wanting, in my opinion, in one of the important elements of a true home.—Boston Transcript.

CHAMPION IRON FENCE COMPANY,

KENTON, OHIO.

The Largest Iron Fence and Railing Works in the United States.

—— SPECIALTIES: ——

Iron Stairs and Jail Work,

Builder's and Ornamental Iron Work,

And the only manufacturers of Malleable Iron Cresting, guaranteed against breakage.

—— Also manufacturers of the ——

Celebrated Ohio Champion Iron Force and Lift Pumps.

In Europe the feeling that the first essential of a refined home is privacy is carried rather too far, for the high walls with which gentlemen's houses are so often surrounded are a sad drawback to the beauty of the country in general, but I believe the principal is a right one.—Boston Transcript.

An Iron Fence is an Essential of a Refined home.

Send for 166-page catalogue.

"It has been wisely said that a well cook meal "civilize the wildest of men."

Among the many things needed to prepare a well cooked meal none is more necessary than a good cooking stove. We present a cut of the famous

JEWETTS WOOD COOK STOVE.

These stoves are made from the very best material, and for elegance of design, and good cooking and baking qualities cannot be surpassed by any stove made. You will find these stoves on sale at the popular Hardware Store of

ROBINSON & SPELMAN,

Who carry a full line of Cook Stoves, Heating Stoves, Gasoline Stoves, Stove Furniture, and a full line of House Furnishing Hardware.

East of First National Bank   KENTON, OHIO.

SASH, DOORS, BLINDS,

SCREEN DOORS, ETC.

GARDEN HOSE, LAWN MOWERS,

SILVERPLATED KNIVES, FORKS & SPOONS,

And everything kept in a first-class hardware store.

AGRICULTURAL IMPLEMENTS,

Of all kinds.

BUGGIES AND CARRIAGES.

Pipe and Fittings for Natural Gas a Specialty

West Side Square,   KENTON, O.

J. S. FRY & SONS,
BRISTOL, ENGLAND,
— Manufacturers of —
Highest Grade CHOCOLATE & COCOA PREPARATIONS

FRY'S PURE CHOCOLATE,

Half pound cakes, each wrapped separately, UNEQUALED FOR ALL DOMESTIC PURPOSES, making cake and candy, or anything in which Chocolate is used, and as a beverage.

For sale by leading retail grocers and at wholesale by

AUSTIN, NICHOLS & CO.,
Importers and Wholesale Grocers,   NEW YORK.

HAPPY THOUGHT SOAP

Excells all others for the Laundry. It is pure, full weight, and can always be relied upon for its cleansing qualities.

GLORY SOAP

Has no equal for Toilet purposes or the Bath. It is absolutely free from all impurities. Nicely perfumed, and leaves the skin soft and smooth and in a perfect healing condition.

Buy your household goods at the

FIVE AND TEN CENT STORE,

— Where you can find everything in —

TINWARE, GLASSWARE,

QUEENSWARE & KITCHEN UTENSILS

Of all kinds at one-half the prices charged by other stores.

5 & 10 CENT STORE,

East Side Square,   KENTON, OHIO.

FOR THE BEST LINE OF

STAPLE AND FANCY GROCERIES,

Fruits, Vegetables and Canned Goods,

— CALL ON —

J. A. MATTLER,

North Side Square,   KENTON, OHIO.

For an entire outfit for the kitchen, in the way of

Stoves, Dishes of all kinds,

Knives, Forks, Shoe Brushes,

And anything in the house furnishing line can be had at one place and the only place in Kenton is at

C. C. BIDDLE'S.

East Side Public Square.

IKE WESTON.   ED. CRANSTON.

— The Old Reliables —

WESTON BROTHERS & CO.,

GROCERS,

West Franklin Street,   KENTON, OHIO

Oysters and Fruit in Season.

Good Goods, Large Stock, Fair Dealing.

Capital, $135,000.00   Surplus, $10,000.00

Depositors Furnished with Safety Deposit Boxes.

OFFICERS:

A. LETSON, Pres.   HUGH L. RUNKLE, Cashier.
N. AHLEFELD, V. Pres.   JAS. H. ALLEN, Ass't. Cas'r.

DIRECTORS:

A. LETSON,   N. AHLEFELD,
JAMES YOUNG,   Wm. YOUNG,
D. W. SULLIVAN,   J. M. WHITE.

CORRESPONDENTS:

New York—American Exchange National Bank; Western National Bank.

Philadelphia—Penn National Bank.

Cincinnati—First National Bank; Third National Bank.

Cleveland—Ohio National Bank.

1ST NATIONAL BANK OF KENTON,

KENTON, OHIO.

OFFICERS:

S. L. HOGE, Pres., H. W. GRAMLICH, Cashier.
J. S. RICE, V. Pres. H. BORN, Jr,, Ass't Cashier.

Prompt attention given to Collections.
Exchange furnished on all parts of the world.

METELLUS THOMSON,

DRY GOODS,

KENTON, - OHIO.

A LARGE STOCK OF

Dress Goods and Silks,

NEW GOODS RECEIVED DAILY.

A force of seventeen Experienced Salesmen and Salesladies always ready to Show Goods.

Your early attendance at our counters solicited.

METELLUS THOMSON,

DRY GOODS,

One Price. C. O. D. - KENTON, OHIO.

www.ingramcontent.com/pod-product-compliance
Lightning Source LLC
Chambersburg PA
CBHW022113160426
43197CB00009B/999